THE SEAMAN'S WORLD

THE SEAMAN'S WORLD

Merchant Seamen's Reminiscences

selected and introduced by
RONALD HOPE

HARRAP  LONDON

in association with
THE MARINE SOCIETY

For
Dorothy English
and
Kay Evans
who together have done much
to encourage seafarers thus
to express themselves.

First published in Great Britain 1982
by HARRAP LIMITED
19–23 Ludgate Hill, London EC4M 7PD
© *The Marine Society* 1982

ISBN 0 245-53893-3

Designed by Robert Wheeler

Printed and bound in Great Britain
by Book Plan Limited, Worcester

Contents

Introduction

These essays, chosen from those submitted for The Marine Society's annual competitions, span some sixty years of seafaring. They are so arranged as to order the events described more or less chronologically, and they thus provide a kind of social history.

At the beginning of this period, in the years immediately following the First World War, the sun never set on the British Empire, and Britain was still by far the world's major maritime power. No seafarer could be unaware of these facts. On his route to the Far East there was evidence of Britain's wealth and power in every port, and the Royal Navy was still very much in evidence. Palatial buildings housed British governors, British banks and British business houses, and round every corner was a romance that Conrad knew. A 10,000-ton cargo ship might carry a crew of 100, plus a dozen passengers, and there was a good chance that they would spend several days in every port of call.

Of course, this was not the complete picture. At Paddy West's in Liverpool casks with both ends removed were suspended horizontally and gently swung. When you could shovel coal right through the swinging barrel without it touching the sides you were a trained stoker, one of the 'black gang' who would sweat it out, watch-and-watch, for 84 hours a week, with a chance that you would lose the job if you took your annual fortnight's leave. At sea you would be given one tin of condensed milk to last three weeks, and you stopped the holes in the tin carefully with wooden plugs after each use to frustrate cockroaches. Fresh meat was carried in an ice-box, but it assumed a greenish tinge after a month, and even when the cook had sponged it down with vinegar it retained an odour of decay.

Change in all this came slowly. It was presaged by the cook who in 1919 spotted an apprentice joining his ship and cried to a shipmate, 'Oh, look at Lord Ginger! Hey, hey, Jack, come an' look at this! Marchin' up the gangplank carryin' bloody suitcases! Ho, ho, ho! Where's yer brass buttons, me lord? Sailors with suitcases! Gawd!'

The days of the seabag and the donkey's breakfast were numbered;

but forty years later I met an apprentice who had been turned off the bridge of his ship when he ventured there for the first time after being at sea for no less than two years. 'What are you doing on my bridge?' the master roared. The luckless youth replied that when he signed his indentures he had thought that instruction on the bridge was part of his training. 'Get off, get off', was his only reply, and he went sadly back to his chipping and scraping of the bulkheads—cheap labour still in 1959.

But, as John Moody points out in these pages, it was the Second World War which initiated major change. Oil replaced coal, the 'Queens' rendered yeoman service, the British Raj began to falter, the T2 tankers were built in the United States, and the sacrifice of merchant seamen was proportionately greater than the sacrifice of lives in any of the armed forces.

After the War the seaman's life was never what it had been before 1939. The seaman fed better. He was better housed. His leave increased. His pay improved. And for thirty years there was no dearth of jobs. After 1960 he might even find women aboard a tanker or a dry-cargo vessel.

'Down Tanker Alley' is a far cry from 'Conrad Country'. But you never get anything for nothing. The seaman's job has become lonelier, for crews are one-third of the number they used to be, and passengers have virtually disappeared. Nor are there many of those glorious runs ashore that sailors used to know. Nowadays you may see more of the world on the package holiday you take on leave than you do in your job at sea.

One factor, though ever-changing, remains paradoxically constant: the sea itself. Captain Evans's log entries aboard the *Phemius* in 1932 inspired Richard Hughes to write his classic sea story *In Hazard*, and a hurricane is still the same fifty years later. Stanley Simpson's epic wartime voyage is only different from the more recent voyages of the 'boat people' in that Stanley was a professional sailor and understood his element. And Captain Gregson's rescue of the missing mess boy — which earned him a Royal Society of Arts award — took place only the other day.

As the old Greek writer Antipater of Sidon observed, perhaps a century before Christ, 'Pray who will for a fair passage home . . . the sea's way is the sea.'

RONALD HOPE

My First Day at Sea
Alec Gracie

I shall never forget joining my first ship. The First World War had been going on for over three years and the submarine menace was at its worst, one out of three British ships falling victim to the U-boats. Although most of my relatives were in the Merchant Service I had not decided to go to sea from any desire to fight nor because of an inborn love of the sea. My great wish was to travel — to see the world. And as the £100 necessary to become an indentured apprentice, together with the cost of uniform, was beyond my parents' means, I signed on as an ordinary seaman on *Poplar Branch*, one of Ritson's turret ships, of Sunderland. There was no particular reason for my choice. The Marine Department of the Board of Trade had offices in Canning Place, next to the Sailors' Home in Liverpool, with two large rooms devoted to the engagement and discharge of ships' crews. On a board displayed outside the building were written the names of any ships that might be signing on or discharging crews during the day. And the first name I saw was *Poplar Branch*.

I was to receive £6 10s. per month and I was given an advance note for one month's pay. I also arranged for my mother to draw half-pay after I had worked off the first month. I was required to join the ship two days later on the 15th October, 1917, at five minutes past midnight. This rather peculiar time for starting work was explained to me later as the method by which the shipowner got a full day's work out of you, as one's working day started at midnight on any day. With my advance note, I left the shipping office and bought from an outfitters in Paradise Street a canvas sea-bag, a straw mattress (donkey's breakfast), oilskins, seaboots and two suits of dungarees.

In what seemed an incredibly short time, I joined the ship in the Alexandra Dock, in the north end of the Liverpool dock system. I arrived aboard an hour and a half early and found that the fo'c'sle was aft, under the poop, and reached by means of a scuttle and a steep flight of wooden steps. At the foot of the steps on one side was the fo'c'sle door, and on the other side was the door of the room shared by the boatswain and the carpenter. Later I was to discover that another scuttle on the poop led down to the Chinese firemen's fo'c'sle and also to the room used by four Chinese sailors. I changed into my working gear and had an hour in which to find myself wondering why I had got myself into this predicament. Somehow, the atmosphere seemed at once depressing and claustrophobic.

The fo'c'sle was rectangular and was built athwartships with two portholes on the starboard side and a skylight (always canvas-covered) built in the deckhead. Lining the room were six pairs of wooden bunks, and wooden benches lay alongside the lower ones. A very narrow wooden table filled the centre of the fo'c'sle. This had two holes, one at each end, and the table slid up and down two steel stanchions. It was fixed at the required height by means of wedges.

My feeling of foreboding was made acute by the sudden opening of the scuttle and the arrival of two large men, both drunk, who asked me if there was any 'effing char' about? When I nervously replied that I didn't think so, they started in a surprised sort of way and took no further notice of me. One of them, rooting about in the nest of small lockers, found a large bottle of pickled onions and they stuffed a few into their mouths, saying they were just 'the gear' for putting them right! While they changed their clothes, the rest of my future ship-mates came down, some accompanied by friends seeing them off. All had bottles of beer that passed from mouth to mouth, helping, I supposed, to make the strain of parting easier. The fo'c'sle was now impossibly crowded with huge bodies and the air reeked with the smell of beer, strong pipe tobacco and Woodbine cigarettes. All this added to the original heavy odour of fresh paint and disinfectant made the atmosphere pretty awful and I wished that I was home again.

Suddenly, over the din, could be heard the sirens of the tug-boats come to tow us out into the River Mersey, and a couple of minutes later a voice shouted from on top, 'Down below there, all hands on deck; single up — and get a move on'. A sudden silence was broken by 'Oh, go and fill yourself', or something of that ilk, followed by a titter of laughter. This was followed by the sound of someone crashing down the ladder and yet another big man appeared, broad-shouldered, blue-eyed and with a heavy moustache, who shouted, 'Who said that?' 'I did,' replied a sailor and he was immediately hit in the face with a blow that sent him reeling against his mates.

'Now, lads,' said the big man, who proved to be the second

mate, 'let's have no more of this nonsense. There's work to do. Get up that ladder, the whole bloody lot of you, and single up.' It was astonishing how the 'crowd' suddenly changed from a bunch of drunks into efficient seamen.

I clambered up on deck with the others and got in the way while the tugs were made fast and the mooring ropes were reduced to the minimum required for casting off. The 'seeing off' parties went down the gangway which was then winched aboard. Soon we were moving away from the dock with the tugs towing us out to the river. The winches rattled as the ropes were brought in. A man was sent to the wheel. I did not take an active part in anything and was feeling very much out of things when the second mate spotted me and said, 'You're making your first trip, aren't you?' 'Yes, sir,' I said. 'Well, you're wanted on the bridge. Get up there and report yourself. Say the second mate sent you.'

I found my way to the bridge. Of course the whole business of leaving port was done in darkness, as it was wartime, and all I could see on the bridge were the dark shapes of a man at the wheel, an officer at the telegraph and two other figures staring ahead into the blackness. I stood uncertainly by them until one of them said, 'Yes? What do you want?' I said that the second mate had sent me. 'Ah, yes,' said the Captain. 'So that's where you were. Well, now, keep a sharp lookout from up here on the bridge. What you're looking for are submarine periscopes or floating mines. Look at the water and you'll see a sort of ripple on the waves end up in a white feathery spray. That's what you normally see, boy. But if you see a white, feathery line moving along as if a stick was being dragged through the water, well, that could be a submarine's periscope. And you'll tell me at once. Understand?' I said, 'Yes, sir,' and although I couldn't really see in my mind's eye what I was looking for I stood where I was told and stared hard at the black water on the port bow.

About half an hour later someone came up on the bridge and spoke to the Captain who, a moment later, came over to me. He said, 'What's your name and who the devil are you?' I replied, 'Gracie, sir, and I'm an ordinary seaman.' He seemed a bit fed up with me. 'Well, why the hell didn't you say so? You've no business up here. Get down at once and report to the Bosun.'

Mystified, I left the bridge and found the Bosun. He didn't seem to like me much either and told me to go and turn in. I learned, a day or two later, that the second mate had been ordered by the Captain to send the new apprentice to the bridge to go on lookout duty. For some reason he had taken it for granted that I was the first tripper apprentice, who, equally bewildered and, of course, clad in dungarees like myself, was sent to the fo'c'sle with the other ordinary seamen. They soon found out the officer's error and sent the apprentice, a Sunderland boy called Henderson, on deck to get himself sorted out by the Bosun. An interesting feature of this episode was the Old Man's kindly talk to me in the wing of the bridge in my guise as apprentice, explaining how to identify a periscope feathering through the water, and his sudden change of manner when he found he was speaking to a new fo'c'sle boy.

I was tired and a bit dispirited. I had spoken to nobody and, except for helping to coil rope and hanging a fender over the side when leaving the dock, had done nothing but avoid people who wanted me out of the way in a hurry. I went down into the fo'c'sle and opened up my bag. Four men were getting ready to turn in and two other boys were sitting on a bench smoking. I took out my pyjamas and was just putting the trousers on when one of the men said, 'What the bloody hell is that you're putting on, son?' They all stared at me when I said, 'Pyjamas'. A couple laughed, but a third man said seriously, 'You don't wear them things here, son. That's all right for officers but it's wrong gear for the fo'c'sle. Just wear your drawers and singlet. It saves time getting into your cart and out of it, as you'll find out for yourself.'

So I did as he advised and that is how I started my years of life at sea.

The Black Gang
Edward Carpenter

Before the advent of oil fuel the crews of all ships included a complement of firemen and trimmers, their numbers varying according to the tonnage and boiler capacity of the ship. Collectively they were known as 'the black gang', and they worked in such conditions of heat, dirt and back-breaking toil that few ashore, with the possible exception of miners, could comprehend them. Even miners went home every night, but the black gang in a tramp steamer might be on the go for a year or more.

Most of the black gang drew an advance of pay when signing on — and joined the ship with a hangover. But they had to turn to in watches set by the second engineer on leaving the berth. A succession of steel ladders known as the fiddley led down through the engine-room to their domain in the stokehold. Here they had to tend the fires.

In most ships the firemen were responsible for three fires, two high and one low. At the end of each watch one of the fires had to be prepared for cleaning out by a process known as 'burning down'. The cleaning was the first duty of the new watch, who had to clear the fire-bars of foreign elements or clinkers.

Trimmers were different. They worked in the hot, airless bunkers where, in a gloomy atmosphere thick with coal dust, they filled steel barrows with coal and wheeled them into the stokehold. Here they dumped their loads on the 'plates' or steel decking below the furnace mouths. There were other bunkers, on the deck above, where the coal was tipped into hoppers, which resembled lift shafts, leading down to the stokehold floor. Inside the bunkers coal was gradually cleared back towards the rear bulkheads, which meant that eventually the trimmers had to cover a longer distance. The floor would be strewn with different-sized lumps of coal so that the barrows had to be wheeled along narrow planks placed in position across the steel decking. This was called 'being on the long run'.

After changing watches, the first task following burning down was to dispose of the raked-out ashes and clinker fragments which littered the deck. Short-handled hammers were used to break them up, then the barrows would be filled and their contents emptied into the 'blower'. The blower was an open metal receptacle to one side of the stokehold into which was tipped the broken-up debris. From it a connecting pipe led to the side of the ship, and by way of this pipe water pressure forced or blew the waste material into the sea. This procedure was known as 'shooting the ashes'. During the First World War U-boat commanders sometimes took advantage of this procedure to stalk their prey and attack — often round about four o'clock in the afternoon when they were also helped by the early evening light. With some furnaces not at full blast, engines would be unable to increase speed at short notice, and so the ship was handicapped and became easier to overhaul.

While the trimmers were shooting the ashes, the firemen would also be busy. First, the burned-down furnace was fed with a 'pitch' of small coal — about a dozen shovelsful. This was known as 'coaling the bars' and gradually the fire was worked up to full capacity. For the purpose of gripping shovel handles or hot steel implements a hand-rag was used, to prevent burns. This consisted of a small, square piece of canvas — or carpet, if this could be procured from the catering department — which was grasped in the left hand.

Meanwhile, other firemen would be stoking up. First, the draught lever had to be pushed over before opening the furnace door. If this were not done, a searing flame was liable to shoot out across the stokehold. A pitch of coal would then be thrown on each fire and the door slammed tight. This stoking up demanded a fair degree of precision as the furnace opening was only just wider than the shovel, or 'banjo' as it was called. If the banjo's edge struck the rim of the aperture it could cause a painful jar to arm or shoulder, besides spilling the coal.

The coal was allowed to burn for a while; then it was time for the 'rake' to be used. This was a ten-foot-long steel implement, similar in appearance to a garden hoe, and with it the spread of coal was levelled off. After another short spell the slice was brought into action. This heavy steel poker — weighing about forty pounds — was driven under the burning coal, which was thus lifted several times to allow the air to assist combustion. The point of the slice was forced upwards, usually by leaping up and bearing down on the handle with the stomach muscles, a strenuous task which could become very tiring towards the end of a four-hour stint.

The temperature down below, especially in the tropics, could rise to anything between 120 and 140 degrees Fahrenheit. A few were overcome sometimes by heat exhaustion, but they soon recovered after a short spell on deck. Burns were unavoidable at times — the affected skin area would then be smeared with a liberal application of black tartaric acid ointment. Thick leather boots and an old pair of trousers were mostly worn in the stokehold, but the trimmers in the bunkers sometimes wore boots and nothing more. The multi-purpose sweat-rag was always tied loosely round the neck, and was in constant use for wiping perspiration from the face and eyes and for clearing lips and nostrils from a clogging, sticky accumulation of sweat and coal dust.

On the whole, food was fair and adequate, though complaints were common during a protracted voyage. In passenger ships the black gang fared somewhat better than their mates in cargo vessels and tramp steamers. Large trays of unconsumed food left over from the first-class saloon dinner would be collected from the galley every evening by the firemen's 'Peggy'.

There was no ice chest for general use, and butter became a liquid mess. Tinned condensed milk and poor-quality jam were issued at regular intervals. Haricot beans, dried peas and lumpy tapioca pudding, all indifferently cooked, were favourite dishes. Maritime regulations enforced a twice-weekly issue of a stodgy plum pudding which was called Board of Trade duff. Cockroaches abounded in the food lockers, and fresh vegetables were rarely seen. Potatoes were stored in open-air lockers, usually on the poop deck for coolness, but more often than not the heat reduced them to a pulpy, tasteless mess.

Crew accommodation was always for'ard under the fo'c'sle head, the firemen and trimmers usually on the port side and the seamen to starboard. One large compartment housed most of the black gang, a long fixed table and wooden forms running down between the two-tier bunks. A number of metal lockers for clothing and working gear were situated alongside another bulkhead. In rough weather the quarters were often flooded out and sea water mixed with coal dust would swill about on deck below the lower bunks. Lifelines were sometimes rigged along the main deck to enable men to reach the engine room in safety. Since all the portholes were screwed up tight, an unpleasant stale body atmosphere pervaded all enclosed parts of the ship. Not all parts of the crew quarters were wired for electricity, so candles stuck in the tops of empty beer bottles were a not uncommon means of light. Washing was done in the fo'c'sle wash-house, and just before the end of each watch a trimmer would come up and fill several buckets with hot fresh water. Sweat-rags would be used as flannels, and then wrung out and used for drying off.

Conrad Country
Stanley Algar

In the 1920s I was second mate aboard a small Shell tanker based on Balik Papan, an oil port on the east coast of Borneo. From there we traded to ports in Malaysia, Sumatra, Java, Seram and the Philippines. It was a pleasant life in what was still Joseph Conrad country. We visited ports that the larger ships could not enter, and many of the places were so obscure that most sailors had never heard of them.

The Captain possessed an extra master's certificate but he was not a comfortable man to sail with. A passion for making voyages shorter than they were said to be in the official distance tables had already caused him to lose one ship, but his confidence was in no way abated. Sometimes he would come on the bridge just after midnight and lay off a course on the chart to pass some unlighted point at a distance of half a mile. He would then declare: 'And on a reef she came to grief, my God!' And he would turn in, leaving a slightly unnerved young watchkeeper to look out for reefs, rocks and sandbanks. Once when he did this, as we were steaming along the north coast of Seram, I altered course five degrees away from the land when he was gone, and put the ship back on his course five minutes before I was relieved by the mate. Currents there could easily set the ship inshore by half a mile. This problem apart, the voyages were tending to become a little monotonous when we were ordered to load a small parcel of diesel oil for Ambon and a few hundred cases of kerosene for Banda. None of us had ever been to these ports as they were normally the preserve of the Dutch company KPM.

We left Balik Papan, headed south down the Macassar Strait, rounded the southern tip of Celebes Island, and headed east into the Banda Sea. Ambon proved to be a small port with a tiny wooden wharf and we had to pump the oil, slowly and carefully, into a wooden tank. The town possessed a large garrison of Ambonese soldiers who were fiercely loyal to the Dutch but, leaning on the ship's rails, the first accents I heard were broad Lancashire. Although we were the first British ship in Ambon for a quarter of a century, the man with the Lancashire accent was there every three years selling Lancashire cotton. The Chinese agent's family had been there for three hundred years; and the 'natives' were not from Java, as one might suppose, but from New Guinea, where the people are darker than the native Indonesians.

Leaving Ambon in the evening, we arrived off Banda at eight the next morning. We missed the entrance the first time because it was so narrow, and when we found it we proceeded cautiously because the channel, although deep, was enclosed to port by the low-lying island of Banda and to starboard by the peak of an extinct volcano. The volcanic island seemed bare of any vegetation, but Banda island was a riot of colour.

As the town came into view the red roofs and white walls of the houses combined with the bougainvillea, hibiscus, orchids and lush tropical vegetation to produce a blaze of flamboyant colour. Equally striking was the spice-laden air wafted to us by the offshore breeze. Nowhere had I seen and sensed anything so beautiful.

When we anchored, the sea too seemed anxious to enrapture us. The waters were so clear and sparkling that I could follow the anchor chain many fathoms down to the sea-bed, where the sand was fine and white and the fish plainly visible.

When I went ashore in the small boat the coral below the surface was plainly visible in a variety of delicate shades of pink and white, as dainty as filigree or lace. Swimming in and out of the coral were small fishes and once again someone had run amok with the colours. Some fishes had bright spots and others had bizarre stripes, like tiny rugby football shirts.

There were two officials in the port, a Dutch harbour-cum-postmaster who doubled as head of the customs and an Indonesian chief of police. So far as they could remember, no British ship had ever been to Banda before. However, whatever our nationality, no work was to be done that day for the chief of police was getting married and we were all invited to the wedding.

We met the wedding party on its way from the mosque to the house, for the ceremony itself had been concluded. Leading the party was a brass band, a collection of rugged individualists who insisted on blowing their own thing. 'Yes, we have no bananas' seemed to provide the underlying theme of the first piece. It was followed by another musical epic dimly recognisable as having something in common with 'It's a long way to Tipperary'. The

British had undoubtedly arrived. After the band came the happy couple, the policeman in his uniform, his bride in white.

After the happy couple came the village notables, the ladies mostly in European dresses and the men in dinner jackets. Some of the dinner jackets were so old that they were green; some of the trousers were so short that they displayed a generous length of calf; and others, made for Europeans with middle-aged spread, could have encompassed two of their slimmer Indonesian wearers. The comedian of the party wore a huge winged collar which may well have been old when Queen Victoria celebrated her diamond jubilee.

After the village notables came those in native dress, their coats and sarongs both bright and gay. The high spirits were contagious and we joined the party and followed those who went before into a large well-built house with an imposing terrace, impressive pillars and a profusion of marble.

The house was not unique. There were many such handsome houses, largely empty and slowly decaying, their neglected gardens a riot of colour and perfume, their Indonesian inhabitants smiling and friendly. How was it that such grand houses could exist on a tiny, out-of-the-way island?

The answer was a simple one. Banda was once the centre of the spice industry. Fortunes were made from the cloves and nutmegs in which Banda seemed to have something near a monopoly. The spice merchants of Banda grew so rich that their ships outward bound, after discharging their oriental spices in Europe, would load marble in Italy for those merchants' grand houses. But the spices began to be grown elsewhere, and they became less significant in the European diet, and the merchants of Banda left their island and their miniature palaces to those who had once served in them.

It was a romantic place for a wedding reception, this decayed mansion of a merchant prince. We drank fresh lime squash or Coca-Cola — for no alcohol was served by these strict Muslims — and the food was the Javanese rijsttafel, the most delicate and delicious of oriental cuisines. Soon the tropical night closed in and the music began, western in one room and oriental in another, the young clutching one another and the old keeping each other at arm's length, as the native custom was. My bazaar Malay was scorned by one young princess who spoke charming English which she had learned in Java, but it proved a happy, friendly occasion nevertheless.

We sailed the following day. It was all a long time ago, but the memory is as brilliant and scented as the reality was when I was second mate.

Cargoes
Denis Chadwick

In the heyday of tramp shipping the handling of cargo had a greater effect upon the lives of seafarers than it usually does in these days of fast modern ships fitted with all kinds of sophisticated equipment.

To begin with, there was the dirty and heavy work connected with coal bunkering. Bunkering was always associated with flying dust which reached all parts of the ship, both inside and out. In the United Kingdom the coal was tipped into the bunkers in ten-ton loads, often from a height, but elsewhere the chutes and grabs were equally dust-raising and dirty. Almost invariably the ship left the bunkering port with many tons loose on deck — to be shifted down as space became available below in consequence of the efforts of hard-working firemen and trimmers. This work was done with a will, for everyone was keen to clear the decks and get the ship clean again and there was great satisfaction when the job was finally completed: at least the dust could be washed away and clothes washed clean. When oil bunkers first came in there was many an overflow when bunkering, and this mess was far more difficult to clean up, leaving stained decks and ruined clothing.

Occasionally, when the ship had a long ballast voyage ahead, coal was also carried in a cargo hold, from whence it had to be shifted to the bunkers as these were emptied. This entailed still heavier work, plus the noise of working winches disturbing the peace.

In those days, Britain's coal exports, although below the peak figure of 77 million tons achieved in 1913, were still considerable — in 1938 they still amounted to 38 million tons — and they provided work for many tramp steamers. Most of this coal went to bunkering ports throughout the world and abroad ships were bunkered almost entirely by hand. Old seafarers will remember the Port Said workers running up and down the gang-planks with their small baskets of coal but achieving quite astonishing loading tonnages. Chief engineer officers had first to go aboard the lighters to measure the coal bulk in an effort to estimate the tonnage they were to receive.

Coal was also exported from other countries and carried in British ships, Durban being one port notable for loading and bunkering. South African coals had a dangerous propensity for spontaneous combustion and fires developed and ships were lost, but mostly the fires in the bunkers were not serious. Wisps of smoke would be seen coming from the surface; attempts, which seldom succeeded, would be made to dig down to the seat of the fire; water would be hosed on, and pumped out of the bilges when it had drained through the coal; and eventually the firemen and trimmers would come across masses of clinker and ashes as they worked through the bunkers.

Grain was a clean cargo, although when loaded in bulk there was a lot of dust. A bulk grain cargo meant the erection of heavy shifting boards on the way to a loading port, a big job sometimes under heavy weather conditions. Grains and seed in bags were easier, but despite careful sealing some always found its way into the bilges. Cleaning this out was a particularly unpleasant task as drainage caused germination and rotting and this, together with the odd dead rat, created a most appalling stench. Linseed seemed particularly bad, and the so-called 'linseed poultices' were really foul.

Gunnies or jute bags formed a large part of the cargo from Indian ports, the rest being manganese ore, tea (the sweepings from this cargo were a welcome improvement on the ship's supply), desiccated coconut and various spices. The odour from a shipment of cinnamon still lingers in taste and memory. Loading in eastern ports was carried out by coolies who practically lived on board, large containers of curry and rice appearing for their meals. They wore a minimum of clothing, but always found stowage for the pouch of betel-nut 'makings' which they chewed continuously, expectorating the red juice everywhere.

Before the tanker trade developed, all petrol and kerosene was shipped in tins packed two to a case. This case-oil was a frequent and important cargo from United States ports, many thousands of cases being loaded at great speed. In New York this was done from lighters in slings, and the dockers were expert at using winch drum ends with rope hoists, saving time by literally whipping the empty hook out of the hold, over their heads, and back into the lighter for the next sling, the winches running continuously. At Port Arthur in Texas an interesting helter-skelter gear was used, the cases being assembled, filled and carried to the top on an endless belt from which they started their run down into the hold to be stowed in place. On one occasion a cargo of this case-oil was loaded together with roofing felt and other temporary building material for Yokohama after their great earthquake in 1923. America had been particularly anxious to send relief, as Japan had been the first to send relief to San Francisco after their 1906 earthquake. In Yokohama, hundreds of ships were anchored in and near the harbour. The empty petrol and kerosene tins became the standard all-purpose bucket in many areas of the world for years afterwards.

Bulk salt was an occasional cargo from Red Sea ports. Massawa was one of them — the hottest known place on earth, its average temperature day and night throughout the year being 86°F; its nearness to the sea prevented the rapid cooling at night which occurs in inland desert places.

For bulk salt, thorough cleaning followed by lime-washing of holds was necessary. This was another unpleasant and even painful job, as the lime on perspiring bodies burnt. Massawa was so hot that the salt was scraped in the evening from salt pans flooded in the early morning. There was no air-conditioning, of course, and any work other than absolute essentials was almost impossible.

During the subsequent voyage to Rangoon the salt packed down hard, and the coolies discharging it would dig straight down, making a pit in the hope that small collapses would ease their pick and shovel work. The collapses were not always small. Occasional bigger ones would lead to shouts, and a rush of labour from all over the ship in an effort to dig out the buried victims before they expired. The heavy salt tax of those days made salt a precious commodity. Sikh guards kept a close watch for pilferage and before lighters left the ship the crews were made to smooth over the surface of the salt, which was then stamped with a large, heavy teakwood die, leaving a patterned surface which would reveal any attempt at pilferage.

Phosphate rock from various Pacific islands was another frequent bulk cargo. At Nauru in the Gilbert Islands it was loaded from surf-boats carrying two large baskets filled from a tip on the reef. These were emptied from the top of the hold, raising a heavy dust, but also leaving lumps of rock on deck which were useful for fishing in a manner peculiar to the island. Large shoals of yellow-tail swam round the ship, but could only be caught by wrapping a baited hook with galley garbage round a piece of rock. The fish would not touch a baited hook without the added attraction of the garbage floating around.

At Nauru the ship was moored to the bottom in 170 fathoms, using a slip-on ship's cable to attach to cable suspended from a buoy and to special anchors. When working cargo, the stern was hove round parallel to the reef by a rope to a buoy on the reef. The boats were towed out by heavy motorboats, which cast off some distance from the ship, leaving the Chinese helmsmen to steer alongside — often with a resounding crash which brought a picturesque flow of language from the Australian stevedore which it was perhaps as well that the Chinese could not understand. These phosphate cargoes were discharged mainly in Australia at works where the phosphate was treated with sulphur to become superphosphate fertiliser. As the crude sulphur was treated to become sulphuric acid at the same works, the ship had to endure the strong fumes.

Another cargo during the loading of which we could never feel clean was the copper pyrites which we sometimes loaded at Morphou Bay in Cyprus. This had a sulphur content which clogged the nose and irritated the throat. Day and night for about a week the loading went on, a week of noise, of clattering winches, and of earthquake reverberations as the two-ton skips tipped the ore down our five holds. Only extreme tiredness allowed us sleep. The discharging of this cargo was always a bone of contention in home ports. The dockers at first used handkerchiefs about their mouths, and then demanded masks. In Liverpool they refused to handle the cargo, but our maritime superintendent had an answer to that. He had a barrel of beer cradled on deck and employed our trimming gang — all six-foot Irishmen who usually trimmed our coal bunkers — to discharge the cargo. It is still a legend around Alexandra Dock as to how many barrels of beer the black-leg Irishmen consumed to discharge that cargo. Nowadays such subterfuge would result in a countrywide strike of dockers.

Of unusual cargoes that come to mind, I particularly remember the 50 tons of dogs' excrement which we took from Antwerp to the Middle East for fertiliser, and the holdful of slaughterhouse bones we loaded in Beirut. Once, in the old ice-box days, we had a consignment of bagged figs from Izmir. Some were stacked ten feet high on number four hatch, just abaft the engine-room, and from these streamed hordes of maggots in endless procession. We had to keep a hose going continuously to keep the wretches from invading our ice-box and devouring our meagre rations.

Hurricane
D. L. C. Evans

On 4th November, 1932, weather reports received aboard the Blue Funnel ship *Phemius* indicated that a hurricane was positioned eastwards of us. It was said to be travelling WNW, of small intensity and sixty miles in width. I altered course to give the storm a wide berth, and during the night the barometer rose steadily.

At six o'clock the following morning the wind freshened and the barometer started to fall. At about 7 am I altered course to give all reefs to westward a wide berth. The barometer continued to fall and at 9 am, with the barometer recording 29.55, I hove to.

By noon the wind was increasing, the sea rising and the barometer still falling. It was clear that the storm had not been in the position given or it had re-curved. All loose gear about the decks had been secured.

By 2 pm the wind was hurricane force with terrific squalls. Up to noon the ship had behaved splendidly but it now fell off unmanageable. After two o'clock the wind became indescribably violent and visibility was reduced to nil by flying spray. The first damage was the blowing away of the bridge apron, the loosening of dodgers, and the smashing of the wheelhouse windows. All endeavours to heave-to were of no avail and the direction of the sea could not be ascertained because we could not see anything. Judging from the motion of the ship, the sea was very high.

By 3 pm the wind had further increased to a force which was beyond conception. I had reduced speed at noon and now put the engines on 'Slow', as no power could cope with this wind force. About this time, during a few moments' lull, I saw some wreckage close alongside and some dark objects flying in the air. These were our Number 2 hatch covers. I ordered the pumps to be put on Number 2 hold at once. At 3.30 pm Number 6 hatch was stripped, some hatch covers remained secured but the rest were blown overboard.

Nothing more could be done to Number 2, so I ordered the Chief Officer to try and save Number 6 hatch as much as possible, and some of the hatch covers were saved. The wind force was so great that the party were unable to return for some hours.

No heavy water had been taken on board up to this time, but the force of the wind carried an almost solid sheet of spray over the weather bulwark on the port side. This spray, striking on the tarpaulins at the edges of the hatch coamings, caused the tarpaulins to be carried away as if cut with a knife. The ship yawed in the sea from 4 to 6 points, bringing the wind from right aft to about two points abaft the port beam. She was rolling very heavily but the quick jerky rolls satisfied me as to her stability. About 6.55 pm I left the Chief Officer in charge of the bridge as I wished to see for myself how things were going in the engine room.

While I was going down the engine room a steam pipe burst in the stokehold — this was taken to be a super-heat pipe. Main steam started to go back, and fumes and smoke came back into the engine room. There was no doubt that those working there were doing their utmost in most difficult circumstances.

On reaching the deck I was caught in choking smoke which I found came out through the fiddley. On looking up and around to seek the cause of this, I found the funnel had gone. As it was then approaching 8 pm, the funnel must have disappeared about 7.30 pm while I was in the engine room. The Chief Engineer did everything in his power down below but conditions were so bad that every effort produced no results.

I went down to the saloon to see for myself how things were down there. I found the saloon awash and all the rooms on the starboard side flooded, a pitiful state of affairs. I then returned to the bridge and tried to estimate the force of the wind. Putting my arm out into the wind I found that the force of the spray striking my hand was agony, and for some minutes afterwards it was numbed as if by a severe electric shock. My estimate was that the minimum force of the wind was 200 miles an hour.

At 9 pm the steam failed, fires blew out with the back draught and oil ran out through the furnace doors. The ship was in total darkness. A constant, almost solid, sheet of spray, but no heavy water, continued to blow over the open hatches throughout the night and I estimated that ten tons an hour went down the open Number 2 hatch and five tons an hour down Numbers 1 and 6 hatches. We were now without fresh water.

During a temporary lull — the dead centre of the hurricane —

at 1 am on 6th November we secured the hatches as well as we could, but we were unable to obtain stores. At 4 am the hurricane centre passed over, the wind increased to force 12 and the sea was very high and dangerous. These conditions continued until 9.30 am when I decided to send out an SOS requesting assistance. Since our aerial had gone with the funnel, the SOS was sent out on the emergency radio.

SS *Ariguani* replied at 10 am and this helped me to keep everyone cheerful, but I realised now that we were being carried along by the hurricane. Throughout the day the engineers tried to raise steam but they had no success. We were now feeling the need for food and water. Burning oil ran out of the furnace doors but was put out by fire extinguishers. Soundings were taken of holds where possible. Throughout the night the ship had been rolling and lurching very heavily. She was carrying a heavy starboard list and at times was taking a starboard roll of 38 degrees. Our position was very serious since no pumps could be used.

At 4 pm we went through the centre again and during this temporary lull all hands tried to secure Number 2 hatch with awnings. By 5.30 pm the gale was again increasing and continued thus through the night. The barometer showed signs of rising at one point, but fell again, and by midnight the hurricane had again increased to a fury.

By 7 am on 7th November Numbers 2 and 5 hatches had been stripped again. We secured Numbers 2 and 6 during a short lull at 8 am but by 9 am the wind was again blowing with violence. The ship was now rolling more heavily and shipping water but so far no large volume had entered the hatches. All attempts at sending out further wireless messages failed because the wireless room was wet and the set was 'earthing' as a result of excessive water. This gave me further concern since I realised that everyone was anxious. The barometer had fallen further and the ship was rolling dangerously. Lee water carried the starboard gangway away and it dragged the rails with it.

Conditions were unchanged at noon and the seas were tremendous. At 1 pm I observed that the ship was in soundings and I realised that we were passing over a reef. The wind was SSE and blowing with terrific violence. The ship's head was ENE, making our heavy listed side, starboard, the weather side. Oil had been got ready in the latrines for this situation. The sea was immense and threatened to engulf the ship. I gave the order to keep the oil going at all costs. One sea struck us and I estimated that a hundred tons of water went down number 2 hatch. I gave the order to put on lifebelts. I had ordered a cast of the lead, which gave 60 fathoms, but as the force of the wind carried the lead straight out, I knew this sounding was unreliable. I have to record here the sterling qualities of the Chief Engineer.

By this time we were very much in need of food and water. I realised that if anything was going to happen, it would happen quickly. All possible were stationed pouring oil, and I must draw attention to the splendid conduct of the two midshipmen and the cadet. The difficulties of carrying 5-gallon drums of crude oil to the forward latrines were immense and although the crew, led and assisted by the Chief Officer to get things going, worked fairly well, the three boys mentioned and the Third Mate deserve the highest praise.

The pouring of oil proceeded throughout the night despite crew bruises, exhaustion, hunger and thirst. The Second Officer superintended the aft latrines oil supply while the engineers carried on amidships. Everyone worked hard.

The effect of the oil was almost beyond belief. Towering seas tearing along towards our exposed and listed side crumpled up within ten feet of the ship and, although we could not escape entirely, they landed on board in heavy volumes of dead water. The ship would have foundered had we not poured oil continuously.

We continued pouring oil throughout the day until about 5pm when the wind lulled because we were in the centre again. All hands then tried once more to secure Number 2 hatch with awnings. A little later we took off Number 7 port tank door to try to obtain fresh water. A little water was procured. The tank door was left off to allow the tank to fill from the engine room and stokehold as by this time there were six feet or more of water in the engine room. The tank filled as the vessel rolled and the door was replaced.

The pouring of oil was continued into 8th November with weather conditions unchanged. In addition to those I have mentioned I must mention the surgeon who was always ready and willing to tackle and assist with anything. About 5.30am I observed the ship to be in deep water by the colour of the sea. The barometer had risen only to fall again throughout the day. At noon the gale was still strong and the sea very high but about 2pm the wind lulled and we were in the centre again. All hands tried to secure Number 2 hatch with boards and awnings.

As I have made clear, the ship was several times in the centre of the hurricane. At these times the ship was overwhelmed by birds and insects, both large and small. Large birds of the heron species landed on the ship in such numbers that I considered it possible that they added to our danger — we had a dangerous enough list without adding to it. The decks, bridge and other areas were crowded with small birds and it was impossible to

walk without crunching some under our feet. They landed fear-
lessly on our bodies wherever they could. The heat was oppres-
sive in the dead centre and it was very quiet. These were times to
test the nerves. I waited patiently for the blast that I knew had to
come from the opposite quadrant and was glad when it came,
carrying with it to destruction all those birds and insects. During
these times I had seen sharks, but kept this to myself.

About 3 pm the wind shifted from SSE to SW, again increasing
to hurricane force. Later in the evening we opened Number 6
port tank door to try to obtain fresh water but obtained very
little. This tank was also allowed to fill from the engine room. I
now estimated that there was over 1,000 tons of water in the
holds and engine room.

During all this time I would not allow the refrigerator to be
opened since once opened everything would be destroyed.
Water and biscuits saved from damaged lifeboats were shared
out and it was on this morning that some fruit and vegetables
and cheese were taken from the cooling chamber. The Chief
Steward did all he could. The wind blew fiercely all night but the
barometer showed real signs of rising. At midnight it read 28.72.

By 2.30 am on 9th November the barometer had risen to 29.10
and the wind was also moderating. An emergency aerial was
rigged by 8 am and we did our utmost to gain communication. It
had been an anxious time for everyone during our enforced
silence and I must now record the good work of the wireless
operator. The difficulties he had to contend with were sur-
mounted and he and the surgeon dried out the wireless room
with blow-lamps. On the first sign of a spark I ordered the WO to
keep on sending out our estimated position. We could not
receive with our emergency set but with the aid of a private
receiving set belonging to the Second Mate we learned that ships
had heard us and at 9.30 am we were in touch with ss *Killerig*.

At noon we obtained an observed position of 18°12′N 80°07′W,
having been carried 209 miles N 8° W by the hurricane. On this
day the Third Officer, with lifebelt and line attached, went down
the after store room. The store room was flooded but he was
successful in grasping some tins as they washed to and fro. The
wind had now moderated to a fresh breeze but the high sea and
heavy swell continued, the ship rolling very heavily, with very
heavy pounding on the starboard quarter. This rolling and
pounding continued throughout the night. I was now more
concerned about the action of the ship than when she was in the
storm — the lee lurches were dangerous owing to cargo on the
starboard side absorbing more water. I again gave orders to the
Chief Engineer to get emergency steam going but there were no
results.

By 4 am on 10th November the barometer had risen to 29.70, the wind was moderate nor'-westerly and the swell occasional, though pounding remained heavy on the starboard quarter. The weather was clear and fine and by 5 am we were firing rockets for the benefit of *Killerig* which was due alongside at daylight. I took a star observation at daybreak. At 10 am we sighted smoke bearing N 4° W and this proved to be *Killerig*. I gave him his bearing and he bore down and arrived close to us about 10.45 am.

Towed by *Killerig*, the battered *Phemius* made for port, arriving in Kingston harbour at 4 pm on 12th November.

Captured by Chinese Pirates
A. D. Blue

It began with the Manchurian Incident of September 1931, when the Japanese marched into Manchuria, ostensibly to restore law and order. If the country had been unsettled before, however, this certainly failed to improve matters. Banditry had long been endemic in Manchuria, but shipping had been unaffected; and unlike on the South China coast, piracy was unknown in northern waters. It was a bleak place, and unpopular with China coasters. When the *Nanchang*, on which I was second engineer, anchored off the Liaotung River on the morning of 29 March 1933, it was my second visit to Newchang, the second largest port in the country, after nearly five years on the coast.

Shortly after breakfast that morning, as we were waiting for the pilot to take us up to Newchang, we were attacked by two large junks, and four of us — mate, second mate, third engineer, and myself — taken prisoner. It all happened with the speed we associate now with the combined operations of the Armed Forces. One minute we were in the saloon, the next down in the dark hold of a junk. In between we had heard gunfire on deck, rushed out to investigate, met a group of Chinese firing off wildly, and been hustled over the side into a large junk. We were more surprised than frightened, and Hargrave, second mate, was highly indignant because a bullet had gone through his sleeve. Johnson, the mate, was more concerned about the radio set he had just bought in Shanghai. We were all agreed, however, that we would soon be back on the *Nanchang*. This just couldn't happen to us.

But it had happened to us, and for almost the next six months our activities more closely resembled strip cartoons than life in the Merchant Navy. For the first half of this time we lived in the junk, and for the second ranged the countryside by night, hiding in farmhouses and hamlets by day. It is this second half I remember more vividly, although the first may have been more exciting. During this first period there was our attempted escape, and our undignified return when we found ourselves in danger of drowning by the rising tide in the mud flats where the junks were hiding. This was our most frightening experience, and the anger and threats of the bandits next morning, when they discovered from our clothes what had happened, failed to worry us any further. A few nights later, Pears, third engineer, was taken away with a letter to the authorities to open negotiations for our release for a ransom. He soon returned, as there were too many soldiers around. He was taken away the next night, and left at the railway station, from where — after some adventures — he made his way to Newchang. Then there was the attack by other bandits, whose prisoners we became. They attacked just after dark, and we had an anxious time wondering how the outcome would affect us. Our relations with the original bandits had improved with time, and we were being allowed to go on deck occasionally and not kept down in the dark and dirty hold for the whole day. During the next few days, when we were only allowed on deck for a few minutes at a time, just to relieve ourselves, we found that our new captors numbered over one hundred with six junks, compared with about two dozen and two junks of the first lot. This second lot were also more hostile, and it took quite a long time for our charm and diplomacy to make our relations with them bearable. By the end of the junk era, however, we were allowed on deck for a few hours each day, and were even cracking jokes with them.

The last exciting event on the junks was the fight between bandits and soldiers which forced us to abandon the junks. For a few days planes had been flying over us, sometimes very low, and we felt sure that our hiding place had been discovered. Whenever a plane approached we were hustled off the junk into the tall reeds ashore, and that night would move down one creek and up another a few miles away. Our sphere of operations was the creeks and mud flats around the north shore of the Gulf of Liaotung. This forenoon, after more than the customary plane activity, when all the junks were anchored up a wide creek, we were suddenly fired on from one bank. The bandits returned the fire, but it increased so much that they decided to abandon the junks. In the confusion of swimming and wading ashore to the other bank, Hargrave and I managed to escape. I was recaptured an hour later, and Hargrave soon afterwards. Johnson had been too closely watched to escape, but his relief when we rejoined him almost made up for our disappointment.

The next few days were the worst of all. With the junks our food had been lost, and we were harried round with very little to eat or drink, and pestered by flies and mosquitoes by day and night. We had been captured in cold weather at the beginning of spring, but it was now mid-June and very hot. One of us alone could hardly have survived this period unharmed, mentally if not physically. Together, however, the dangers, discomforts and threats did not worry us unduly. We felt sure we would not be killed in cold blood, as the bandits would then have nothing to bargain with, and they still hoped to get a good ransom for us. Our greatest danger came from accidental bullets, when the bandits were cleaning their guns. They were monumentally careless, and Hargrave had had a second narrow escape.

After a few uncomfortable days, our captors decided to break new ground, as our area of operations was getting too hot for us. We set out one evening after dusk, over a hundred of us in single file, each of us with a rope harness round his shoulders, and one of our bodyguard at each end of the rope. It was not a particularly irksome form of restriction, but very effective in preventing any attempt at escape. Strict silence was the order of the night, and we marched until morning, crossing the railway line and enter- ing farming country in the early hours. This was a severe strain on us in our weakened condition, but was a wholesome change from skulking and starving in muddy creeks. Our shoes had given out long ago, and we were wearing cloth shoes. Hargrave had cut his feet in our second escapade and they soon caused him trouble. His persistent Yorkshire grousing, however, brought a donkey, and he finished the journey on its back. Soon after crossing the railway line we halted in a clump of trees outside a hamlet, and everyone lay down exhausted. If we had had any strength left we might have attempted to escape, but we were too tired and weak even to suggest this.

Next morning we had a pleasant surprise — unlimited boiled eggs and 'pings' for breakfast. These latter were like large pan- cakes, and for most of the time were our main food. Baked with a little oil they were not unpalatable. This morning a dozen or so eggs with a few pings made our best meal since we had been captured. We usually — like our hosts — drank hot water for safety, but on this occasion a clear cold spring had been found, and a drink of clear cold water rounded off our meal.

After another similar meal in the evening we repeated our performance of the previous night, and this was the pattern of our lives for nearly three months, although there were no more mara- thon walks as on the first two nights. We usually set out at dusk, and with a few short halts walked until midnight, which took us to our next hiding place. While we waited outside the selected hamlet an advance party went ahead and prepared the way. On following them the gang would split up into groups of about a dozen, and each group would be billeted in one farmhouse. The farmers were always friendly, and we lived comparatively well during this period — plenty of vegetables, with an occasional meal of pork. Under such conditions our health improved quickly, and we were soon almost back to normal.

We had always wondered who was the bandit chief. We knew that the leader of our bodyguard was small fry, although he always tried to impress us with his importance. One night when assembling for our march an unusually well-dressed bandit approached us. Negotiations for our release had been going well at the time, and relations with the bandits were comparatively good. This man asked us how we were getting on, and assured us that we would soon be back among our friends. He was obviously someone of importance, and our guard said he was the real Number One.

It was about this time that we had a haircut. For once we were marching through the day, and came across a barber when passing through an unusually large village. In the prevalent mood of good nature he was summoned, a stool brought, and each of us in turn given the full works — haircut, beard and moustache trim, nose and ear cleaning. The appreciative audience of bandits and villagers did not detract from our enjoyment of this gala event, and we felt wonderfully refreshed afterwards.

During this period of marches and counter-marches there had been several letters and parcels from the authorities at Newchang. Among the cigarettes, Bovril, soap, and so on had been a small English-Mandarin book. This had greatly helped with our language problem, and thus our relations with the bandits. We could talk fairly fluently, if not grammatically, with our captors, and Johnson was even trying to learn Chinese characters with a painstaking earnestness which would have pleased Samuel Smiles or Dr Albert Mansbridge.

The memory of these night marches sometimes comes back to me as clearly as if they had taken place a few weeks ago. We normally avoided villages and hamlets as much as possible, but sometimes a dog barked, and would be answered by every dog for miles around. Then the villagers would join in beating drums and gongs to frighten off marauders, and for a short time it would be bedlam. Mostly our marches would be quiet, however, and, after the long hot days in squalid farmhouses, invigorating and soothing.

Although we were separated when marching, we came together at the halts, when we discussed everything under the sun or moon, from our prospects of freedom to a review of the situation in Manchuria, China, and the world at large. It was like those long rambling discussions between Tom Sawyer,

Huckleberry Finn and Jim, when drifting down the Mississippi on their raft. A constant topic was how our handing over would be effected, and the bandits collect a ransom without being captured. There seemed so many possibilities of treachery on both sides, with ourselves as losers in any such attempt. When — after a long period of delays and postponements — the handing over took place, it was something of an anti-climax.

One forenoon we were taken into a large farmhouse and left there. A few minutes later several Japanese and Manchukuo soldiers entered and told us that we were free men, but must remain there until darkness. This would allow the bandits to divide up the ransom money and disperse their various ways. There were only some two dozen soldiers in the rescue party, so that treachery would be likeliest from the bandits. Everything went smoothly, however, and at dusk we found a farm cart outside the farmhouse ready to take us away, with an escort of mounted soldiers. Some of the old friends in our bodyguard had remained behind to bid us farewell. They were going home for the winter they said, to live on their share of the ransom, and would reunite in spring for another similar operation. We were assured, however, that we would not be molested should they meet us again.

A ride in a farmcart seemed an undignified end to our adventures, but the five-hour ride to the town of Panshan passed agreeably, if not comfortably, in discussion of our first meal and night out in Shanghai. We slept — fitfully — in the officers' mess in Panshan, after sharing a meal of tinned salmon and biscuits washed down with innumerable toasts in saké with our rescuers. Early next morning we boarded an armed railcar for Newchang, where we were officially handed over to the British Consul-General. Then we went to Grant's house for a late breakfast, bath and haircut. Grant was our Newchang agent, and he made us more than welcome. It was now 8 September 1933, and our Manchurian adventure, or misadventure, was over.

Mugged in Buenos Aires
J. N. Dickinson

It was carnival time in Buenos Aires and the President's palace made a brilliant show. No less brilliant were the profusely decorated avenues that lead into the Plaza Mayo; while packed almost to suffocation with carefree humanity out to do justice to the occasion, the Plaza itself was a riot of colour. Señors and señoritas of all shapes and sizes, in every description of fancy costume, gaily saluted all and sundry with brightly-coloured streamers and confetti, while picturesquely-dressed policemen looked on with indulgent smiles. It was an occasion which any stranger would be foolish to miss.

Stepping blithely down the gangway of ss *Marbelton* on this particular Saturday evening in mid-summer I felt as gay and lighthearted as any of the huge throng of pleasure-seekers boisterously making their way to the main scene of the festivities. The Old Man had very decently granted his crew a few pesos — a pound a head — with which to go ashore and join in the fun, and each of us had donned his Sunday best for the occasion. Being happiest when wandering around on my own, I had waited until the rush was over and was the last to go ashore.

The evening's programme as set out in my mind was to visit one or two of the big cafés that line the Arcade, have a couple of beers and listen to the music, and then make my way to the Plaza Mayo, concluding perhaps with another beer in one of the expensive-looking cafés adjacent to the President's palace before returning to the ship.

And so, according to plan, I found myself at midnight sitting at a table in the Café Americano partaking of a farewell glass of beer. In my own quiet way I had spent an enjoyable evening. I had bought some streamers and confetti and joined with gusto in the game of throwing confetti at my fellow pedestrians and streamers at the gay señoritas parading the Avenida Mayo in their cars. My amusement had been quite innocent and as I paid my bill I inwardly congratulated myself on the cheapness with which a steady-going fellow could enjoy an evening of carnival in Buenos Aires. I still had seven of my ten pesos left.

After the brilliance of the Plaza Mayo and the neighbouring Arcade, I found the way to the docks dark and a trifle lonely and I suffered grave misgivings when, halfway on my journey, I was accosted by two nondescript figures desirous of knowing the way to Number 3 Dock. One of them, a medium-built fellow who proved to be a Maltese, was looking for a Prince Line ship, and the other, a tall, well-made man badly in need of a shave, was supposedly a Swedish bosun. Their explanation was that they had been drinking and had lost all sense of direction.

Knowing that a Prince boat was berthed in Number 3 Dock not a great distance from my ship, I took this explanation in good part and invited them to accompany me to the docks. Coming to a particularly dark stretch of road, with only warehouses on either side, the conversation, never more than desultory, suddenly ceased and I experienced a feeling that all was not well. I turned round to discover the cause of this sudden quiet and at that moment the big Swede jumped on my back and bore me to the ground. I gave a yell and kicked out with all my might but was swiftly overpowered. In less time than it takes to tell, the two rogues had gone through my pockets, taking my money, a wallet containing private papers and a souvenir brooch I had bought for my girl. They finished up by seizing my wristwatch and forcibly divesting me of my raincoat, following which, with a farewell kick in the ribs, they disappeared in the direction of the city.

As I picked myself up, bruised and sore, two mounted police, who must have heard my cries, galloped up and demanded to know what was wrong. As best I could, and mainly by signs, I explained the robbery and described my assailants. Commanding me to stay where I was, they whipped their mounts and set off in hot pursuit, and it speaks well for their efficiency that within ten minutes of the hold-up they were back with their prisoners, the Maltese and the big Swede, complete with my raincoat, seven pesos and a wristwatch but, regrettably, no wallet or brooch.

A voluble conversation now ensued with the Maltese, who could speak Spanish fluently and made vehement protestations of innocence, the upshot of which was that the three of us were invited to the nearby calaboose. I felt no misgivings at this invitation since, with an interpreter in attendance, I assumed I would be able to prove my case and so regain my property while the two rogues each received a well-merited term of imprisonment. My dismay may be imagined, therefore, when, safely lodged in the calaboose, I, along with my assailants, was charged with being drunk, fighting and disturbing the peace. Strong protestations notwithstanding, I was marched along a narrow corridor and thrust unceremoniously into a filthy cell already lodging a round dozen of the most unsavoury characters Buenos Aires could produce.

In this cell I lay all through Sunday with no-one to heed my appeals, with no-one to note my sorry plight and with only a crust of hard, dry bread and a small can of water to allay an ever-increasing hunger and thirst. There was nothing but the pleadings of the poor wretches incarcerated with me who, though they could speak no English, clearly wanted a cigarette to relieve the deadly tedium of this unhealthy dungeon.

Early on Monday morning I received a visitor — none other than the Maltese who shared responsibility for the desperate situation in which I found myself. He looked so dirty and ill-kempt that at first I could not be sure that it was he, but a scar down one side of his face, of which I had taken particular note, proved his identity beyond doubt. Had I had a knife I would have killed him, for I was half crazy with hunger and my long sojourn in that hell-hole. As it was I took rough hold of him and, my hands around his throat, made as if to strangle him, but he begged pitifully for mercy and asked me to listen while he explained the why and the wherefore of our close confinement.

He then told me that the prime instigator of the hold-up was the big Swede, who was a beachcomber and one of the city's most lawless characters. He himself, he was at haste to explain, was a genuine seaman serving on a Prince boat and, but for an unfortunate meeting in a dockside dive and the fact that he had partaken of more drink than was good for him, would never have been party to the robbery. When charged — principally to save himself from a term of imprisonment, for he was married to a girl in Cardiff and had two young children — he had told the official in charge that the three of us were friends who had been spending the night drinking together and had unfortunately quarrelled on the way to the ship. The raincoat, he told the police official, was actually mine, but the money and the wristwatch, which he pointed out would in all probability be confiscated, he had said were his own and all in all it had been nothing more than an unfortunate squabble about nothing in particular.

At the conclusion of this tale I found myself at a loss to know what I should do. I failed to see how I could prosecute the man for the police were inclined to accept his version of the affray and were in no way disposed to trouble about me or my insistent demands for an interpreter. Then, if his tale were true, he had been an unwilling accomplice, and to press the case further would be to bring hardship and unnecessary suffering upon his wife and family in far-off England.

I tried to be stern. 'Well', I said, 'when will we be released?'

'Today, brother', he replied. 'In about an hour's time we'll be driven along with these other unfortunates to the stables to clean up the stalls, following which we will all be kicked out into the fresh air and told to vamoose, pronto. That's the reason why I've been marched into this cell alongside you. They've kept the big Swede back for a week or two because they know he's a bad character and only a taste of solitary confinement will curb his activities.'

And so it came to pass. Along with the Maltese and the other weekend drunks and disturbers of the peace, I was marched through the damp and evil-looking corridors to the stables and promptly commanded to clean up the stalls, following which the gates were thrown open and we were assisted, with many boots, to freedom.

I should have mentioned that, prior to the stable-cleaning episode, the Maltese and I were ordered to the charge-room to receive back 'our' personal belongings. The Maltese received the wristwatch and four pesos and I was presented with a torn and soiled raincoat. Back in the cell, the Maltese, afraid of what might happen otherwise, handed over the watch and the four pesos.

But such is the brotherhood of the sea that, when the prison gates were far behind us, I invited him into a little wayside café and we both did royal justice to a good breakfast. He left me at the entrance to number 3 Dock the richer by a packet of cigarettes.

Atlantic Convoy
Frank Goodall

Ss *Oiltrader*, my second tanker since the war began, was a fairly fast ship — a good thing when sailing alone. I joined her in the Mersey where she was 'gas-freeing' and that night we moved down to the Bar. Merseyside was being hammered by the Luftwaffe and *Oiltrader*, shown up by the light of flares, was attacked but not hit. Next morning we anchored off Cammell Laird's shipyard where funnels and masts sticking out of the water indicated that others had not been so lucky.

We sailed in a slow convoy. It was much the same as usual: routine signals, alerts, and one tangle with U-boats. Soon, in the Western Approaches, we broke off on our own and steered fantastic courses to try and fool the submarines. A couple of weeks later we made St Nicholas on the island of Aruba in the Dutch West Indies. The place seemed open to attack from seaward and we heard later that a half-loaded tanker at the wharf where we loaded was torpedoed on the berth.

We loaded 16,000 tons of octane and sailed alone, with orders to join a convoy east of Nova Scotia. Safely through the Caribbean and past the Antilles, we pushed northward into the Atlantic. One day something big headed our way. We manned the 4·7-inch gun, tested the Hotchkiss and slipped a grenade into the Holman projector. These were the nerve-pricking minutes that really bothered us — waiting for action.

It turned out to be a grey Cunarder come to shepherd us into the convoy fold. Within the hour a destroyer raced towards us and someone said, 'The Navy's here!'

Oiltrader joined a big convoy and we were in distinguished company. The battleship *Ramillies* squatted in our midst for Winston Churchill was with us. *Oiltrader* was in the starboard column and just abeam of her cruised an enormous French submarine.

The weather was fine for some days. At the end of each day,

when the western sky was all reds, greens and golds, and the gently moving purple sea looked as if it had been squeezed from some gigantic wine press, Wullie, who came from Barra, would bring out the chanters of his bagpipes and play the haunting melodies of the Isles.

Steadily eastward we moved, not a light showing, everyone alert. And the day came when the wolf-packs first harried us, and the convoy shuddered to the blast of a torpedo dead on target. Then we heard the thunder of depth charges and sporadic gunfire. When the dawn came up Number 10 was gone and Number 31 was a flaming hulk.

So it went on for several days, with U-boats beaten off only to return to the attack, and each day the convoy pushed on further to the east.

As we neared the Western Approaches the weather worsened. From signal halyards bunting hoists stood out stiffly, and the leaden-hued sea hissed and snarled along the side of the ship. The nights were dark and moonless and this was just as well because now we were approaching Focke-Wulf territory.

Then the fog came down and all that we could see of the ship ahead was the grey plume of water thrown up by her fog buoy. Radar was new then and only fitted to the Commodore and to the naval escorts. A hundred ships groped blindly in the dark, with the danger of collision ever present. But at least the U-boats were blinded too.

Suddenly a big tanker, not of our convoy, barged through us on the opposite course. She and an ammunition ship met almost head on, grinding past each other with tortured steel screaming and sparks being thrown off in showers. The smell of octane came from the tanker and we tensed, waiting for both octane and ammunition to blast destruction all around. But the ships came apart and sailed on, and soon the fog lifted again.

One morning a horned mine bobbed past *Oiltrader*, and a few minutes later we passed another one. But worse was to come, for, later that same morning, smoke poured from the magazine — there was fire in the ammunition.

Volunteers rushed aft, ventilators were covered and steam was forced into the magazine. I remember looking aft at the rising smoke and the scurrying men and feeling that in some way it was all remote from me. The ship could blow up and many die, but not me. I suppose it is this lack of imagination which makes it possible for men to face up to terrible danger.

Slowly the smoke thinned until the last wisp dissolved above the mainmast truck. We never learned how the fire started, and *Oiltrader* in station steamed on.

Now we met with the first gulls out from home. Around the

ships they wheeled, dived and soared, their beady eyes alert for scraps of food. They were unlucky because during daylight hours a convoy dumped nothing. Flotsam would leave a fine pointer for the enemy.

That morning four-engined bombers, wave-hopping, roared in low between the convoy columns, machine-gunning and sometimes rising steeply to drop sticks of bombs. None of the ships dared to use their ack-ack guns because they were afraid of hitting each other. All at once the Germans made off again, except for one which attacked our Sunderland flying-boat escort. Anxiously we watched while the Sunderland, with the German on its tail, climbed. Suddenly the flying-boat plunged towards the sea and the enemy plane, with guns flaming, dived to make the kill. Then, from under the belly of the Sunderland fanned plumes of spray — once, twice, three times, and she was up, up and rising, while the Focke-Wulf, tricked into that steep dive, crashed into the sea and burst into fragments.

The afternoon of that same day began quietly. The Commodore had worked off his usual after-lunch signals so we hoped he would take a nap and give us a rest from the Aldis lamp and flag hoists. At half-past three the Captain came up the bridge ladder and said, 'Lovely afternoon!'

Just then all hell broke loose. Destroyers tore round in an orderly 'box' and the convoy shuddered to the explosion of depth charges. The din rose to a crescendo, and gradually diminished as our escorts drove the U-boats away from the convoy. Then the destroyers raced back, one, a Hunt-class destroyer, playing *Tally-ho* over her loud hailer. They only did that when they were certain they had made a kill.

Three hours later the convoy pushed through a big area of some clotted brown stuff. A ship had been sunk ahead of us just before the U-boats had made their attack on the convoy.

At last we came to the Minches, and someone pointed out a sheep pen as Wullie's house. Because of a mistake made by one weary quartermaster a ship turned to starboard instead of to port and the convoy became disorganised and had to scatter. When it had been herded together again by corvettes and destroyers the Commodore flew a signal which referred to a passage in the Bible. When we looked it up it read: 'Wherefore like sheep have ye all gone astray?'

We were almost home again. It was not yet *schnorkel* days, when inshore sailing became as dangerous as deep sea. Though still possible, air attack was unlikely because RAF Coastal Command was now active and beside our faithful circling Sunderland screaming Hurricanes and Spitfires gave us heart. *Oiltrader's* cook glanced out of the galley and said to an AB, pointing his ladle skyward, 'I don't know 'ow them RAF blokes do it. Dangerous job that!'

By night we came into the Mersey where the sky sparkled with flak and throbbed to the beat of aircraft engines. Stark against crimson skylines stood the gaunt smoking skeletons of shattered buildings in Liverpool.

Next day we berthed at Port Sunlight. In its way a minor historic moment this, for *Oiltrader* was to open what had been a whole oil installation as an octane berth. Her cargo was just half pumped out when it was as if the earth and sky met in a tremendous explosion. Columns of black smoke spiralled up from the river's bank, a long stretch of which was blown out. Valves were quickly screwed down, connections to the shore uncoupled and the ship taken to Stanlow where the remainder of the cargo was discharged without further event.

The 'Queens' in Wartime
James Bisset

The first word that I was to command the *Queen Mary* came to me in February, 1942, when I had just taken the *Franconia* to Trinidad for fuel and water. The Cunard Company agent came on board and handed me a cable which read: 'Land in Trinidad with your gear and await further orders. Staff Captain will bring *Franconia* home.'

Trinidad seemed a long way from anywhere and I was sorry to leave the old twenty-thousand ton *Franconia*. One grows to love a ship and her crew after three years of peace and war so it was somewhat glassy-eyed that I boarded a launch the next day, said goodbye to the Staff Captain, and left my ship. The launch circled her before heading for the shore and the *Franconia*'s crew gave me three cheers as we went round.

On shore everything was hush-hush. Our agent professed not to know why I had been landed, but the Naval Authorities, after some hemming and hawing, told me as a profound secret that the *Queen Mary* was due in about ten days and I was to be her commander. That the movement of such valuable ships as these great passenger liners must be kept secret in wartime is obvious, but when a vessel has to take on 6,000 tons of oil fuel, 4,000 tons of fresh water and about a thousand tons of consumable stores, and all sorts of advance preparations have to be made to receive her, such as additonal navigational aids, setting up landmarks and laying buoys, the local folk at those places where the 'Queens' were due to call soon guessed what was coming. I expect many lounging longshore-men at Trinidad could have given me the information the Naval Authorities gave me so reluctantly.

As it happened, I did not join the *Queen Mary* at Trinidad but at sea, twenty miles out from Key West where she was fuelling from a tanker. I reached her after a wearying journey, a bus ride and a somewhat rough passage on a small tug. Just before the tug

let go from Key West two young US Naval Ensigns asked me if
they could come out and see my ship, but I do not think they
enjoyed the trip or even saw *Queen Mary*. The captain of the tug,
a hard-bitten old sailor and a fine seaman, told me his cook was
very anxious to have the honour of cooking me a meal and he
cooked a fine dish of steak and chips. I enjoyed it, but I think the
smell of the grilling steak added to the wild movements of the tug
as she drove through a rough sea, shaking every rivet in her and
bringing spray right over, was too much for the young officers.
They disappeared from sight. I felt sorry for them for I had
suffered the same weakness of stomach as a lad.

We found the *Queen Mary* with a tanker on each side and it
was quite a job getting me on board in the heavy sea running.
The tug skipper made a grand job of it, however, and eventually I
got on board my new command. I was met by Captain Townley,
whom I was to relieve. He had reached the retiring age of 63 and
was going home, and not feeling too happy about it. He told me
he had left Boston two days before with the intention of calling at
Trinidad, but owing to intense U-boat acitivity the ship had
been diverted to Key West. She was fuelling out here while two
American destroyers patrolled round her as protectors. Captain
Townley told me that on the previous night ten ships, most of
them tankers, had been torpedoed near his track and he considered himself very lucky to have reached Key West safely.

Having changed into dry clothes and gone over the business of
a changing command, I went on the *Queen Mary*'s bridge to be
introduced to her officers. The bridge rose ninety feet above the
water and projected eleven feet beyond the ship's sides on either
wing, so that one could get a good view along her whole length
from this high position. Standing out there, gazing at my new
ship's massive form, her three towering funnels against the
background of a wild, broken sea and grey mist, I confess to
feeling a great pride . . . and not a little apprehension. When I
took her over she had on board 8,398 US troops, the first ever to
be sent to Australia, a crew of 905, a British and American
permanent military staff of 157 officers and men . . . and it was
wartime. To sink this ship, or her sister the *Queen Elizabeth*, was
the ambition of every German naval officer, for that indeed
would earn him high honour and be a tremendous blow struck
for his country. It was my job, with the help of others who might
never see the ship, to see that this did not happen. That was no
light weight to carry.

During the Second World War the *Queen Mary* and *Queen
Elizabeth* together travelled well over a million miles and carried
a million and a quarter troops. They visited Rio de Janeiro, Cape
Town, Aden, Simonstown and a dozen other ports they would

never have known in peacetime running. They rode a hard war by any standards . . . and without ever sighting an enemy vessel of any sort or firing a shot in anger from the defensive armament. That was a great triumph of ship management, Naval Intelligence, military organisation, navigation, seamanship and marine engineering.

At the outbreak of the war in September, 1939, the *Queen Mary* was on her way from Southampton to New York with a record number of 2,332 passengers and a thousand crew. After an exciting passage she landed them safely and then laid up through the autumn and winter at her pier in New York while the Admiralty and the Cunard White Star Company debated her future employment. Many people thought that to fill her with troops was like putting too many eggs in one basket and that she would present such a wonderful target to submarines and aircraft that they could not miss.

Meanwhile, her sister, the *Queen Elizabeth*, was nearing completion on the Clyde. Her presence there had become a source of anxiety to the British Government for not only did she offer a sitting target to enemy planes — thus endangering the whole of John Brown's great shipyard — but her vast bulk was occupying space that was urgently needed for other work.

In February, 1940, the Admiralty requested that the *Queen Elizabeth* should leave the Clyde at the earliest possible date and 'remain away from the British Isles'.

This was a problem, for the number of ports outside the British Isles that could accommodate the world's largest liner was limited, so it was decided to send her to join her sister in New York. This involved a 3,000 mile journey across the Atlantic in wintertime — notorious for heavy weather — and subject to the ever-present danger of submarine attack. There was no proper three-day trial trip to reveal possible defects in the engine, or to allow several hundred prominent shipping men and journalists to enjoy her luxury in advance of the travelling public. Nothing like that! She just slipped out of the Clyde one dark stormy night in the utmost secrecy and made for New York like a scalded cat. After a boisterous passage she arrived without serious trouble on 7 March, 1940, and tied up alongside the same pier as the *Queen Mary*.

That evening a cable arrived from the Queen Mother — then of course Queen herself — which read as follows: 'I send you my heartfelt congratulations on the safe arrival of the *Queen Elizabeth* in New York. Ever since I launched her in those fateful days of 1938 I have watched her progress with interest and admiration. Please convey to the Captain my compliments on the safe conclusion of her hazardous maiden voyage — Elizabeth R.'

Leaving the *Queen Elizabeth* in New York to get over her

teething troubles, the *Queen Mary* sailed two weeks later for Sydney, calling at Trinidad, Cape Town and Fremantle en route.

At Sydney she immediately began fitting out for troops. This meant the wholesale removal of carpets, pictures, tapestries, wardrobes, furniture, silver and glassware to storage on shore and the erecting of several thousand bunks in all the cabins and public rooms. Working day and night this was quickly accomplished and on 4 May, 1940, she sailed for England with 6,000 Australian troops — her first real wartime job. The journey took six weeks.

Several months later, when she was back in Australian waters again, she was joined by the *Queen Elizabeth* which had been to Singapore for conversion to a troop carrier. From then on the two ships separately made several voyages from Sydney to Suez and England with Australian and New Zealand soldiers.

Their massive grey hulls, distinctive lines and enormous decks, thronged with khaki-clad figures, became familiar sights at Sydney, Fremantle, Suez and Trincomalee and by the end of 1941 they had carried well over 80,000 troops, mostly to the Middle East. So much for the general war service of the 'Queens' up to that time.

The two ships usually travelled unescorted. The reason for this was that destroyers could not keep up with them except in calm weather.

The 'Queens' always travelled at full speed and weather reduced this very little. As soon as a bit of sea or swell developed destroyers began to pitch and before long were burying their noses and sustaining damage while the 'Queens' went serenely on. Speed being the main safety factor for such great ships, the destroyers would be left behind. When it was considered that it might be safer to reduce speed to retain a fighting ship escort this decision was made on the spot. The main protection was of another sort and its excellence is proved by its success. It was mainly good routeing by the British Admiralty and the US Navy Department.

On the day of sailing from any port the captain, accompanied by his navigating officer, radio officer and cypher officer, went ashore and called on the naval authorities. There he was given the exact route he must follow from port to port, the time of departure and expected time of arrival, the speed to be maintained, the latest information regarding the position of submarines, derelicts and icebergs, the position, course and speed of convoys or independent ships that might be met, the latest confidential and secret signal books, instructions for breaking wireless silence and the provision of air or surface escorts. Armed with all this information the captain sailed, and as long as he was able to carry out the instructions, the Navy knew exactly where he was at any moment. If he got considerably out of position because of fog or bad weather he could break silence and report accordingly.

If the Navy got further information about dangers near the ship's track, they sent out secret coded messages giving precise instructions for avoiding the dangerous area. These were called 'diversions' and as many as six of them might be received on a transatlantic trip, altering the distance by several hundred miles. We grew to welcome diversions because they indicated that Naval Intelligence was on the alert. All this, coupled with the great speed of the 'Queens' and constant zigzagging, enabled them to elude the U-boats.

Under no circumstances, even to save life, could the 'Queens' stop at sea, and this rule got a member of my staff into trouble with his wife. On one voyage, leaving Sydney with only sixty passengers, we returned to New York by the reverse route, omitting Key West. Between Rio and New York, when we were in a position about 200 miles north of Bermuda, we sighted five lifeboats loaded with men, also a capsized boat. It was a fine day, with a moderate wind, and the boats were under sail and steering a course for Bermuda. It is a hard decision to make not to stop and pick up brother seamen in distress, but the capsized boat indicated that they were probably near the scene of the disaster and a German submarine was probably lurking around, waiting for just such a thing to happen. I made a signal slowly with a powerful morse lamp saying I would report their position by radio, and regretfully left them. On arrival in New York I got a message from the US Navy Department, thanking me for my prompt action and stating that an American ship had picked them up safely the next day.

A few weeks later our purser, Charles Johnson, received a letter from his wife in which she wrote: 'Our son was in one of those lifeboats and was chagrined to see his father go speeding by, leaving him in the lurch.' The sunk ship was the ss *Lady Rodney*, bound from Halifax to Bermuda with passengers and cargo.

We had our own scares, of course.

On one occasion, when about 200 miles northwest of the Irish coast, a tremendous explosion occurred about a quarter of a mile off on the port quarter. A geyser of water shot about three hundred feet into the air and the engine-room crew reported feeling a heavy concussion. Nothing else was seen and the probability is that a torpedo had been fired at us from extreme range and on reaching the end of its run without hitting anything had destroyed itself — as they were designed to do. All countries in wartime fit this destruction device to their torpedoes so that they will not be picked up by the enemy and their secrets exposed.

On the other hand, as the ship was in soundings — that is, in less than a hundred fathoms of water — the explosion may have been caused by a moored mine of the acoustic type, which is set off by the vibration of the ship's propellers. Whatever it was, we did not stop to investigate.

The organisation of great ships like the 'Queens', the reception, housing, feeding and entertaining of, say, 15,000 troops, was not the least remarkable feature of these ships' war work. The ships themselves and their crews were, of course, the concern of the officers and the Cunard Company, but the troops' welfare and arrangements were handled by a combined British and American staff attached permanently to each vessel. Excellent relations were maintained between those staffs and the ships' officers and crew, and much excellent work was done for the troops. After all, each voyage was like re-populating and then evacuating a small town and each lot of troops had to be instructed in many things they had not experienced before.

To understand the problem that had to be faced and overcome by the combined staff, consider the embarkation of 15,000 troops at New York. On the ship's arrival a conference would be held, attended by representatives of the management, ship's officers, permanent staff, port embarkation staff and military officers, to decide on time and date of embarkation and the berthing arrangements, gangways, meals and many other factors. Three days before she sailed an advance party of two thousand officers and men would embark and they would immediately begin to familiarise themselves with the ship and the duties they were to carry out during the voyage. They included military police, sentries, guides, kitchen porters, mess orderlies, anti-submarine lookouts and extra gunners. For administrative purposes the ship was divided into three areas — red, white and blue.

The main embarkation might then commence at 7pm. The troops would be brought from their camp by ferry boats which landed them on the end of the pier and they would march straight aboard. As he crossed the gangway each man was given a coloured card showing where he would sleep, when and where he would eat, and where he would muster for emergency drills. Guides directed the men to their sleeping quarters and there they had to remain until the embarkation was completed. Loud-speakers throughout the ship announced any orders that might be necessary from the Orderly Room and no smoking was allowed. At 1am the embarkation would be completed, by which

time most of the men had turned in to their standee beds and
fallen asleep, and the order was 'lights out' till 6 am. There were
12,500 standee beds in the ship which meant that when she was
carrying a full load 2,500 of the men had no bunks and had to
sleep on certain reserved portions of the deck. These were
known as the 'overload' and were only carried during summer
months when no great hardship was involved.

Standee beds were an American invention and represented
the last word in troop accommodation. They consisted of two
tubular metal uprights on to which were hinged tubular frames,
each 6 feet long and 2 feet 6 inches wide. Strips of canvas were
stretched on these frames by rope lacings and formed not at all
uncomfortable beds. The beds were spaced far enough apart for
comfort and might be in three or more tiers, according to the
height of the space occupied. In the daytime the beds could be
hinged upwards and secured with a small chain and hook, thus
leaving space for the men to move around. The advantages of the
standees were that they were light in weight, easily cleaned,
occupied a minimum of space and had no crevices to harbour
vermin. The canvas strip was quickly replaced each trip for
cleaning.

With a load of 15,000, about 1,300 of whom were officers, it was
only possible to serve two meals a day. The officers' dining room,
which in peacetime was the tourist lounge, seated 350. The troop
mess hall, which was the first-class dining room, seated 2,000,
and the decked-over swimming pool another 200. There were
four sittings at each meal for officers and six for men. The first
meal started at 6.30 am and finished about 11 am. The second
started at 3 pm and went on till 7.30 pm. The mess halls were
fitted with numbered metal tables and wooden benches and the
tables averaged about eighteen men each. There were two mess
orderlies for each table. They formed queues in the kitchen,
drew the food in large metal containers known as mess kids, then
carried it into the mess hall and dished it out at the table. As each
orderly drew his food he was checked off on a large mess board
showing the number and size of his table, and this prevented
him coming back later for a double dose.

Each sitting lasted about forty-five minutes. There were no
frills, no time wasted, everyone got a good square meal and any
food left over could be taken away if desired. Traffic in and out of
the mess halls was controlled by military police who brooked no
loitering. The story is told of a GI being thrust into a queue and
protesting loudly. 'What's the matter?' asked the MP. 'Don't you
want any breakfast?' 'Breakfast!' echoed the indignant one. 'I've
been shoved in for three breakfasts already.' As soon as a meal
was over the orderlies scrubbed out the mess hall, tables and

benches, polished the mess kids and got everything spick and span for the inspection. Every soldier carried his own knife, fork, spoon, plate and cup, and he had to appear at table for his proper sitting or miss his meal altogether. The men entered the mess hall at one end and left by the other so as not to clash with the queue for the next sitting. As they filed out they were directed by guides to batteries of dish-washing tanks. Each battery consisted of four large tanks in a row, the first holding boiling soapy water, the second boiling fresh water, the third boiling disinfectant, and the last boiling sea-water. The eating utensils, commonly known as 'eating irons', were designed so that they could be all hooked together and held by a long wire handle attached to the plate. As they passed the batteries they 'swizzled' their gear vigorously in each tank, by which time it was as clean as a whistle.

The following is a typical shopping list for one voyage of one ship:

> 76,400 pounds flour, cereal, etc
> 21,500 pounds bacon and ham
> 155,000 pounds meat and poultry
> 4,600 pounds cheese
> 18,000 pounds jams
> 29,000 pounds fresh fruit
> 31,400 pounds tea, coffee, sugar
> 124,300 pounds potatoes
> 31,000 pounds canned fruit
> 56,300 pounds butter, eggs, milk powder

In addition to the mess orderlies the chief steward employed about three hundred troops in getting stores up from the refrigerators, helping the butchers and bakers, preparing vegetables for the cooks and re-stocking the canteens from the storerooms. There were nine canteens — or PX's — in various parts of the ship. Four of them sold soft drinks and cigarettes, and the others toilet articles, candies and other eatables. Prices were low and they were well patronized.

Immediately after the ship sailed — or before if possible — the officers were mustered in the main lounge and addressed by the Staff Captain and Commandant on the subjects of ship's routine, emergency drills, black-out, abandon ship and other important matters, and from then on it would be the officer's duty to see that his men were similarly informed. All hands were then exercised, firstly in air-raid drill when every man took cover in his sleeping quarters below decks, and, secondly, in emergency drill when everyone mustered on the upper decks ready to abandon ship if the signal should be given. The ship had thirty lifeboats that could accommodate three thousand men, and enough liferafts to support another 17,000.

Each man had to wear his lifebelt, properly adjusted, and after that carry it with him wherever he went for the rest of the trip, hugging it to him like a bosom friend. The emergency drills were carried out daily during the voyage, and occasionally at night to accustom the men to moving about in darkness. The only people excused were mess orderlies and helpers, gun's crew, lookouts and sweeping parties. The sweeping parties were organised to cover the whole ship inside and out and were constantly on the go trying to keep the decks and cabins free of cigarette ends and litter. But it was during the emergency drills that they were able to make a good job of it. When the air-raid drill was on they got half an hour to sweep the deserted decks, and when the emergency drill was on they got one hour to sweep out deserted cabins and other sleeping quarters. There were hundreds of litter bins all over the ship but the average soldier seemed to go out of his way to avoid them. During the night the seamen scrubbed and washed the decks with sand and sea-water, except those places occupied by the overload. These were tackled when they moved off at 6 am.

Although the ship was only five days at sea, every effort was made to carry out religious observances and to provide recreation and amusement for the troops. The padre and the Red Cross officers had this in hand. Two movie shows were held daily on the promenade deck which was enclosed and could be darkened. Movies were also shown in the lounge and concerts were held both there and in the large mess hall where a stage could be erected in a few minutes. Plenty of portable Victrolas and records could be had on loan, also a supply of musical instruments such as saxophones, trumpets, clarinets and drums, so that any men who knew how to use them could form an orchestra and entertain — or infuriate — their shipmates. All manner of books, games and puzzles could be had for the asking. The time and place of all religious observances were published in printed daily orders which were available to everyone. Most of the men seemed to sit or stand around just gazing at the sea and probably longing for home. I think it was these men who, to while away an idle hour, carved their initials in the teak-wood rails. At the end of the war there were thousands of them, with hardly an inch to spare.

The ship's hospital, with two hundred beds, had a medical staff of three doctors and fifteen orderlies. It speaks well for the health of the troops that never more than thirty beds were occupied and those only by trifling cases. After D-day, however, for several voyages, the 'Queens' and other large ships were pressed into service as hospital carriers and each carried as many as 2,500 sick and wounded at a time from Britain to America. This meant a large increase in hospital staff and considerable alterations in the way of providing hospital cots instead of standees, and special arrangements for supplying hot meals to men who were unable to walk to the mess halls. At the same time it must be remembered that the ships were still carrying record loads on the return voyages, which necessitated modifying the hospital arrangements both in New York and on the Clyde each time we went there.

It was sometimes remarked in peacetime that ships the size of the *Queen Mary* were 'white elephants'. There was no truth in this, of course, and during the war it was abundantly proved that each of the 'Queens' was worth ten ordinary liners. And further-more, each voyage was a feat of organisation and teamwork, not only on the part of the officers, crew and permanent staffs, but also of the owners and authorities on shore.

To the *Queen Mary* fell the honour of carrying Winston Churchill and his Chiefs of Staff across the Atlantic on three occasions to important conferences in the United States and Canada. These trips took place in April and August, 1943, and in September, 1944. On the first one the Prime Minister landed in New York and returned later by way of a British cruiser. On the second he landed in Halifax NS and again returned by cruiser. On the third he landed at Halifax for the Quebec conference and rejoined the *Queen Mary* at New York for the passage home. On these occasions the Prime Minister travelled with a party of 195 people, which included Mrs Churchill and his daughter Mary. He also took with him Lord Louis Mountbatten, Lord Leathers, Sir Alan Brooke, Sir Ralph Metcalfe, Sir Charles Portal, Admiral Sir Dudley Pound, Admiral Sir Andrew Cunningham, General Ismay, General Wingate and a number of other high-ranking naval and military officers and civilians. The rest of the party consisted of Mr Thompson, his private detective, various secretaries, clerks, typists, cypher officers and a marine guard. The whole party was accommodated on the main deck. The Prime Minister and his family occupied a special suite amid-ships on the port side with a private dining-room for fourteen people, and nearby there were a large conference room and a secret map room. Stretched fore and aft from this were typing rooms, coding offices, numerous sleeping cabins and sitting-rooms, a rest room for the ladies and a lounge.

The map room, in charge of Captain Pim, RNVR, had a chart of the North Atlantic and maps of all the fighting fronts pinned on the bulkheads with special lighting arrangements over them. Mr Churchill would spend an hour here each day studying the

situation in conjunction with all the latest reports. Marine
sentries guarded all this accommodation and no outsiders were
allowed to enter except on special business. The ship, of course,
carried her usual quota of passengers and in one instance had 450
German prisoners sharing the voyage with her distinguished
passengers.

A goodly number of other prominent people crossed with me
during the war and I always made a point of meeting them and
extending whatever courtesies lay within my power. Among
them I remember the then Archbishop of York, Lord Semphill,
Lord and Lady Keynes, Admiral Stark, Admiral Sir James
Somerville, Walter Lippman, Sir Alexander Korda, Sir Thomas
and Lady Beecham, Sir Basil Dean and Malcolm Sargent.
Representing the stage and screen I met Katherine Cornell,
Beatrice Lillie, Constance Cummings, Claire Luce, Brenda
Forbes, Nancy Hamilton, Bing Crosby, Bob Hope, Fred Astaire,
Edward G. Robinson, Douglas Fairbanks, Junior, and Mickey
Rooney. All these good people and their companies were going
to or from the fighting fronts and they had many stirring tales to
tell of their adventures near the lines. They all did what they
could to entertain the troops on board.

I was trooping from the beginning of the war in 1939, first in
the *Franconia* and then in the *Queen Mary*. The responsibility
was heavy and sometimes did not even bear thinking about. I
spent many anxious days and nights but still managed to remain
cheerful and in reasonably good health. The secret of this was, I
think, attention to detail and sticking close to the job. Of course, I
loved the sea and that probably had something to do with it too.

In the early days of the war I used to sleep in my cabin below
the bridge. If I heard hurried footsteps overhead, or excited
voices, or strange sounds, I wondered what was going on and
why I had not been called. This was nervewracking so I decided
to try sleeping in the chartroom, which was right on the bridge.
It had a comfortable settee, reading-lamp, heaters, ventilation, a
window looking out on to the bridge, and I was on the spot if
anything happened. Before attempting to sleep I always took
every possible precaution for the safety of the ship and then had
the comfortable feeling that there was nothing more to be done.

Knowing I was in the chartroom, the officers and men on the
bridge kept quiet, but they knew that if wanted I could be there
in a flash.

I had every confidence in my officers and I believe they had
confidence in me, but the responsibility was mine and it was
their duty, in cases of doubt or difficulty, to call me in time. I
always slept in some old clothes, ready for a jump, and generally
with one eye and one ear open.

After VE-day, when things had returned to normal in the North Atlantic — that is, no black-out, navigation lights burning and no zigzagging — I decided one fine night to undress and go to bed properly in my cabin. Three hours later I was called for dense fog. I went on the bridge and stayed there the rest of the night with the foghorn shattering my eardrums. After that, I returned to the chartroom. I felt happier there.

The 'Queen's' last war job was to bring back US troops from Europe to the United States, fifteen thousand at a time. They were cheerful and goodhumoured and friendly, and I never sailed with better shipmates. One day I passed two GI's who had been making a sightseeing tour of the ship. One said to the other, in my hearing, 'I'll bet the British wish they could build a ship like this.'

On 20th June, 1945, we arrived in New York with the first full load of returning soldiers and had a wonderful reception. Blimps and helicopters flew overhead with loudspeakers blaring out the latest songs. Harbour craft steamed alongside with flags flying and bands playing, and every ship in the harbour blew three long blasts of welcome as we passed, and we returned the salute. The *Queen Mary* was decorated with flags, the ends of the piers were gay with red, white and blue paint, and showers of paper could be seen fluttering down like snow from the skyscrapers. It was certainly a great day for everyone.

In February, 1945, I was knighted by King George VI and received this cable: 'Following from Prime Minister to Commodore Bisset. Please accept my warm congratulations on your knighthood. It well becomes the Commander of such a proud vessel which has played no inconspicuous part in our victory.'

I like to think that these high honours were not for me so much as for the two great 'Queens' and all those who served on board them in the war.

The British Raj
John Chace

Our wartime ML had been built on the Nile and was to be towed through the Sweetwater Canal to Ismailia and then up the Suez Canal to Port Fouad for fitting out.

The Pilot as far as Ismailia was Captain Custa, an elderly Greek, squat and fat, who had been master in sail before going in to Suez pilotage. However, before he was fully qualified, a younger man several places junior to him on the roster had been promoted over his head, whereupon Custa burst into the manager's office, made to that startled official's face a gesture that could only result in Custa's instant dismissal, and then withdrew again shutting the door with such violence that the glass shattered into 'one thousand pieces'. After that, Captain Custa never appeared again on the Suez Canal but, with the war, he was given occasional employment on the Sweetwater.

On another occasion, early in the war, it was reported to Custa that the Italian Consul in Ismailia was in a bar, casting aspersions on the Greeks and their ability to defend their country. Again Custa stormed the citadel: 'Italiano Consul say to me, "Good morning, Captain Custa." I say to him, "Bang!"' (smacking one fist into the palm of the other). 'Teeth – finish. Twenty days in 'ospital!'

His English was not good but several times a day he would say, in a solemn, confidential tone: 'Das Gerrimans' (and here he would spit, with great feeling, into the canal). 'Das Egyptians' (spit). 'Das Italianos' (loud hawking, followed by spit). 'But das Englishmans . . . ah!' And then, slowly nodding his head and with one finger drawing down his lower eyelid, 'My dears, I seen 'em.' At the end of which monologue we would all shuffle our feet and make suitably modest noises.

Such then, was our Pilot, a fine specimen of the old, tough school; always polite and friendly to us, but ready for anything and afraid of no man. With him he brought two young Arab assistants, whose function will be explained later.

After the usual shipyard farewells, we were towed away by a small tug, skippered by a one-eyed villain in a long, dark night-shirt, and our voyage to Ismailia began. Before long we came to a railway bridge and learned that we would have to wait, as a special train was expected bearing King Farouk. Then it was that we discovered the purpose of Captain Custa's two assistants.

The tug slackened speed and guided us close into the canal bank — we were drawing less than six feet — and first Mohammed, at the stern, and then Abdul at the bow, jumped overboard bearing small anchors which were made fast inboard, splashed their way inshore, and secured the ship by digging their anchors into the bank.

A large crowd of loyal citizens began to collect, armed with stones and bottles with which to greet Farouk as he passed by, but as after a while they started to use us for target practice, the authorities decided to open the bridge and let us through.

The tug had not been too easy to control so far, but once he got the bit between his teeth, the Arab skipper became apparently deaf to all directions from the Pilot. After much shouting and blowing of whistles he would eventually thrust his evil face out of the window of the little wheel-house and make some angry comment, but if Custa continued to insist on his orders being obeyed, as he nearly always did, the skipper would often leave the wheel to look after itself and come aft, from where, while Custa continued his harangue, he would call upon Allah to witness that he could not be held responsible for the safe conduct of the Infidels if he was thus constantly distracted.

However, things went well and there were few hold-ups, for Captain Custa was known and feared on the canal and, at the sound of his imperious whistling, the lock-keepers were gal-vanised into unaccustomed activity. However, their efforts to pass us through quickly rarely met with any rewards, other than cries of abuse and threats of the wrath to come if it were not done more quickly next time.

Custa had already told us where he intended to secure for the night, and it soon became evident that he was determined to reach that particular spot by nightfall, in spite of the time we had lost at the railway bridge. Perhaps he had friends living near there whom he wished to visit. At any rate, we pressed on at full speed along the narrow waterway and woe betide any unfortunate Arab craft that came along, for there were no old-fashioned ideas about steam giving way to sail where Custa was concerned.

It was already growing late as we approached the last lock before our appointed resting place for the night. The Pilot blew his whistle, this time with no response, but still he held on. Again the whistle, and the tug skipper began to show signs of alarm as he viewed the rapidly approaching lock gate. 'These men will open gate, Captain,' said Custa confidently, adding meaningly, 'they know me!' But now we could see, through the gathering dusk, that the gates could not open for us because there was already an Arab dhow in the lock.

On the bridge, a vision passed before our eyes of a badly damaged ML, a smashed lock gate, a sunken dhow, the canal blocked for months and perhaps even flooding of the surrounding countryside. Each of us began mentally to compose one of those dread epistles beginning, 'Sir, I have the Honour to report . . .'

However, Captain Custa appeared quite unconcerned. With one wave he stopped the tug and with another wave directed Mohammed to step ashore with his anchor. 'Not so,' replied Mohammed, or as near to it as he could get in Arabic; for to jump into the shallows a few feet from the bank is one thing, but now the ship was in midstream, where the water was comparatively deep, and moving at a goodly pace withal.

Custa turned, with a look of outraged astonishment on his face, as if unable to believe that anyone should refuse such a simple request. 'Hammed!' he bawled. 'Anchora!' Mohammed began to call upon Allah to witness that the ship was too fast, the bank too far and the water too deep — that he would surely drown and who then would provide for his wife and children in Zagzig? But Custa was not one to waste time arguing with subordinates and, with a roar, he lunged at the Arab, who fled screaming.

An ML is but 112 feet long, so the chase was soon ended and a shivering Mohammed cornered at the stern where, with breaking voice, he pleaded for mercy. Standing there, bare-footed, in his torn night-shirt, a small round, woolly hat on his head, and with both hands — one still holding his anchor — clasped to his chest, he presented as heart-rending a spectacle as one would ever expect to see: but not to Custa. Seizing a boat hook, he swung the brass end at Mohammed who, realising that further conversation was useless, uttered a wail and disappeared overboard.

On surfacing, he took one look at the menacing figure still brandishing the boat hook and then despairingly set his face towards the bank, which he reached not without difficulty and, spurred on by threats from the deck, set about bringing up the ship. With the aid of Abdul who, being a bright lad and able to take a hint, soon joined him, he was at last able to stop the ship just a few feet from the lock gates.

We all drew a deep breath and were quite prepared to call it a day, except for Custa, who waited impatiently while his assistants went to find out the reason for the delay. Imagine then his reaction when Abdul returned with the news that 'these men do not want to open the gate'. No doubt the crew of the heavily laden dhow had paid baksheesh in order to spend a quiet night in the lock, secure in the knowledge that none of their competitors could pass them in the race to market.

'Captain,' said Custa to me, for he called us all that, irrespective of rank, 'Captain, bring your pistola.' We had been supplied with a revolver — without ammunition — to ensure our safety on this hazardous voyage, and to the accompaniment of ribald applause from my brother officers, I buckled it round me as we stepped ashore and up to the lock.

We were met by a small party of Arabs whom Custa angrily ordered to open the gates. Loud argument broke out at this but Custa silenced them and, pointing to me, spoke a few sentences to them in a surprisingly quiet voice. It later transpired that he had threatened that not only would I shoot them out of hand but, not content with foreshortening their existence in this life, I would do other things which, according to their religious beliefs, would seriously affect their prospects in the next! At any rate, all resistance broke down and they made haste to work the sluices, raise the little bridge and open the gates. The crew of the dhow awoke to find themselves being warped, willy-nilly, into the canal.

As we made fast for the night in the appointed place, the CO began to compliment Captain Custa on his ability to control the Arabs, but this Custa would not accept. 'I have done nothings, Captain,' he said. 'When they see English officer with his pistola they know he stand no nonsense.'

He paused, to make sure we were all listening, and then said slowly, 'Always, Captain, am I telling: Das Gerrimans (spit), das Italianos (spit), das Egyptians (hawk, spit), . . . but das Englishmans . . . ah! . . . My dears, I seen 'em!'

Voyage to Tobago
Stanley Simpson

I was on the bridge when the torpedo struck. It was the loudest sound I had ever heard. The great column of water threw the matchwood of the outswung starboard boats high into the air and the fall of debris seemed interminable. The ship lurched heavily to port. This — my mind recorded with strange clarity — was what the text books called 'the initial heel', and by the time I had reached the port lifeboats the ship was almost on an even keel again.

The men worked quietly with many white faces but no panic and the two remaining boats were freed and lowered. A hurried census showed many missing: two officers, three engineers, two radio-men, the entire watch in the engine-room, six gunners — nineteen men in all.

I made a quick decision, and was gratified to realise that I felt no pang of fear at this stage.

'I am going back,' I said to the Chief Engineer. 'Take over my boat for a while: lie off and wait for me.'

'You must be quick, Mister,' the Captain called from the other boat. 'She is going fast.'

'Let me come with you, sir!' It was the senior cadet in the Captain's boat. Two days ago he had had his seventeenth birthday. I looked at the Captain and, after a moment's pause, the Old Man nodded his head.

The boy climbed nimbly on board. The ship was, as the Captain said, sinking fast, her stern almost awash. I made for the engine-room and directed the boy to the wrecked cabins along the starboard side. The silence was sepulchral, accentuated rather than disturbed by a sound like water rushing over a weir. It was the sea pouring into the dying ship.

The dark and tangled chaos of the engine-room, thick with the sour stench of the explosive, was obviously nothing but a tomb and the one figure I found was mutilated beyond my aid. I came out to the daylight with a sense of immense relief and met the boy who said no word but simply shook his head. He looked white and sick.

The ship's stern was now completely submerged, and we could feel the deck falling away beneath us. We slipped into the sea and swam away. We had not gone far when a rumbling crescendo of sound drew our eyes back to the ship. It was a wonderful and terrible sight. About a hundred feet of her bow pointed straight out of the sea, trembling under the stress of a thunderous noise, as the great engines, the anchors and cables tore their way through the bowels of the ship — a dreadful sound that scribed ineffaceably deep into the tablet of my memory. Then the bow slid quickly under in a boiling of white foam and flotsam.

Our eyes searched the rim of the sea, and at last we saw the lifeboats afar off, looking very tiny and remote. We swam strongly towards them. At one time I had drawn a few yards ahead of the boy who cried out, 'Don't leave me, sir!'

'Why should I leave you now, son?' I replied, and dropped back to keep pace with my companion. I noticed with increased anguish of mind that the boats were pulling not towards us but away from us — the boat-crews had thought, as I later found out, that we had gone down with the ship, and it was some time before the boats saw us and turned about.

The boy seemed to be tiring and did not speak again for a long while. His next words brought the sour metallic taste of fear to my mouth.

'Oh, Christ! A shark!'

I had known fear before, and was to know it often again, but never such an extremity of terror as that moment. The sleek dark fin seemed to move very slowly through the water. The boy was by this time almost unconscious and vomiting feebly as I towed him towards the boats. There were now three sharks circling us and drawing closer, and the first attack had a nightmare illusion of slowness — no sudden quick rush, but a deliberate head-on approach of indescribable horror. I struck out with my free hand and felt the dreadful solidity of the shark's head as it swirled past, grazing the skin from my arm from wrist to shoulder.

The boy was taken only ten feet from the boat. I did not see him go — a violent wrench as the body was torn from my grasp, a sudden rusty staining of the sea, a confused memory of shouting men and flailing oars as I was dragged into the boat: that was all.

After a few minutes of black nausea, I felt better — and needed to be as there was grim work to do. A man had been found in one of the mid-ship gun-nests almost disembowelled. His mates had carried him into their boat. He was unconscious and far gone as I worked upon him, and he died as the last suture was tied. The boat was overcrowded with the living, with no room for the dead and the body was dropped overside where the grey ghouls awaited it.

The Captain's boat approached and hailed us. 'You seem to have a lot of men in your boat, Mister.'

'Twenty-eight — far too many, sir,' I agreed. 'Close me, then and I shall take some from you,' the Captain said. 'I have only fifteen here.'

I named six of my men for the transfer as the boats drew together. A light breeze had now risen, and the sea which had been almost calm before, developed a certain liveliness. The boats crashed together and then fell away, and one of the allotted men lurched into the sea. He was dragged on board again, terrified but unharmed.

'We have provided enough fun and games for these brutes,' the Captain said bitterly, waving a finger at the sharks that circled like beagles around and between the boats with a horrible eagerness. 'We will keep together for a while — this wind may drop a little later on.'

I took out a chart from its waterproof case and pricked off the boats' position on an ocean that looked deceptively small.

'We are eight hundred and twenty miles from Tobago Island, our nearest land.' I said. 'But it is dead to leeward — we will make it all right.'

'What do you think, Mister?' The Captain spoke after a long pause.

'I think we should sail independently and lose no more time,' I replied.

'Yes — you are right, I think,' said the Old Man slowly. 'Shall I give you some of my provisions?'

I looked again at the slow-moving black fins alongside my boat. 'Let us go, sir,' I said, a surge of sick loathing flooding my being. 'We are losing time.'

Masts were stepped and the brown sails hoisted. The canvas filled smoothly with the freshening trade-wind, and the boats gathered way, heading westward almost into the eye of the setting sun.

The Captain's boat, with its lighter burthen, soon drew ahead. 'Bon voyage, Mister,' hailed the Old Man. 'See you in Tobago!' The boat was already far off when darkness shut down upon it.

It was never seen again.

The men settled down as best they could, and within an hour the boat was quiet, except for the occasional grate of the baler. The moon rose early and revealed the crew sleeping peacefully in every pathetic posture of exhaustion, but I had never felt wider awake in my life. I steered mechanically, keeping the breeze broad on the starboard quarter. My mind was a tumbling turmoil of the events of the day, and the anguish of the boy's death pressed heavily upon me, as it was to do for many days.

I felt a small hand upon my arm, and looked down at the face of the little monkey that snuggled into my side, mewing and looking up sadly at me. She belonged to the Radio Operator — now dead — and was the first into the boat after the explosion, the sailors had said. She still wore the preposterous little life-jacket Sparks had made for her. The gentleness and affection of the creature touched some chord of my emotions and I felt my eyes hot with unaccountable tears, and was glad of the darkness.

In these latitudes, twelve degrees north of the equator, the daylight came and went quickly, and within fifteen minutes of the stain of light to the eastward the sun rose eagerly from the sea. Most of the men were now awake, but some still slept like the dead, curled into a foetal posture of ineffable pathos, and were roused with difficulty. The monkey went from man to man, looking earnestly into their faces and chittering in hopeless query, and there were soon smiles and laughter in the boat — a welcome sound.

I talked with the men, telling them that I was quite sure we would be saved — a conviction I truly felt, and which rarely deserted me during the long weeks ahead. The trade wind, I said, was almost constant in these seas, and set, with the current, always in our favour — we had much to be thankful about. I warned them against likely disappointments — of ships they might see that would pass them by unheeding; and I told them of my plan to make the land under our own sail. But the land was eight hundred miles away, at least a fortnight's sailing in a boat such as this — probably much longer. I voiced most of my hopes, and none of my fears, and asked the men to work for me and with me, and with each other. I was grateful to see not a single dissenting face in all that forlorn group.

The boat's company was divided into two watches, four hours on duty and four off, with routine tasks for the watch on deck — the boat was to be kept baled and clean, the sail and gear to be nursed carefully against wear and chafe. The Chief Engineer was to command the second watch, was to be obeyed instantly and implicitly, and would take sole command of the boat if it so fell to him.

Water and food were served out, and most of the men drank avidly, but several took their meagre four ounces of water only under compulsion. The monkey had her share with the rest, relieving the almost ritual solemnity of the meal with her lugubrious disapproval of the fare, although she later developed a liking for malted-milk tablets, and would unwrap her ration from their wax-papers with comic and childlike pleasure.

The climbing sun became fiercely hot, and a canvas awning was spread for the watch off duty, who took what rest they could, stretched out upon the thwarts, or in the bottom of the boat. The working watch had an unremitting task in keeping the boat free of water, for she leaked heavily and continuously, and the rhythmic scraping of the balers merged into our daily life like the ticking of a household clock.

The most valuable item in the boat was a bag, containing my sextant and tables and elemental data for navigation, which I had kept always packed and ready to hand on the ship. This equipment, with a good wrist-watch that had survived the hazards and immersion of my long swim to the life-boat, provided the tools whereby I could pilot the progress of the boat from day to day — an immense practical and spiritual comfort to us all.

The morning of the third day found us one hundred and thirty miles from the scene of disaster, and the heavy-laden boat lumbering along at three knots before a freshening breeze. Soon after noon the sky astern darkened; heavy towering heads of nimbus climbed to the zenith, covering the sun and thickening at the horizon to a menacing inky monochrome. The lug-sail was lowered and furled, and the conical canvas sea-anchor dropped overboard, pulling the boat's head to wind and sea and none too soon. The sea-rim closed in upon us, and the horizon rushed towards us with a hissing sound. Great drops of water that seemed almost glutinous pattered into the boat like lumps of fat, and in a few moments the full anger of the squall was upon us, lashing us with torrential rain, and tossing sea-water over the bow as the small vessel pitched and strained to the drag of the sea-anchor. Much of this water was shed by the canvas hood that was rigged over the forward half of the boat as some protection against sea and sun to the watch off duty, but we were still hard put to it to rid the boat of the water that rose to our knees in spite of furious baling.

The fury of wind fell away after a time, but the heavy rain continued. Canvas was spread and soon every tank and beaker and receptacle was filled, and each man drank to repletion. Into the short dusk and far into the night renewed squalls and rain rushed down upon us, and I felt thankful that I had not yielded to the first temptation to run the boat before the favourable wind. Yet this relief was tempered by a chafing of the spirit as I thought of the miles and the time we were losing. It was nearly dawn when the last squall went howling away behind us and the stars came out.

The sail was hoisted again, and the boat turned once more to the westward. The daylight revealed a soaked and shivering company but their spirits rose with the sun and in the know-ledge of the filled watertanks. Singing was heard in the boat for the first time since leaving the ship and soon the few shy voices became a chorus in which the whole group joined.

A week later the boat had made nearly four hundred miles towards Tobago. The trade wind had fallen to a light breeze that barely filled the clumsy sail, and the day's run had never exceeded fifty miles. No more rain had fallen, but the store of water was such that each man still received a ration of four ounces three times every day, and there was no sickness in the boat. The food issue had been reduced and the inroads of twenty-nine (including the monkey, whose place and value on the list had never been questioned) gave me some private disquiet during the night watches, when responsibility seemed to press heaviest.

In the satchel that held the sextant was a book of English verse from which I drew solace immeasurable. These magic symphonies of words and mind-images obtained a new lustre, and even poems known by heart revealed, in this atmosphere of private fears and hope and loneliness, a significance and value previously undetected. I read aloud to the men one morning and they asked for more. To most of them poetry had meant the province of the long-haired and effeminate or the stodgy boredom of long-forgotten schoolday verse, and it was good to see the impact of 'The Lotus-eaters' and the 'Ode on a Grecian Urn' upon minds which had been made receptive to the beauty of language for the first time in this crucible of adversity.

On the nineteenth day morning 'sights' showed the boat to be less than a hundred miles from the island. The company was still intact, although five men were so weak and dispirited that they slept all the time and took food with reluctance. More heavy rain had fallen, and it was the ample water ration that had preserved us all. No ships had been seen and the men had often spoken of an obsession that pressed daily heavier upon their thoughts — a sad feeling that this small boatload of humanity was the only life upon a vast and hostile sea. As the boat neared the Indies, I was beset with fears I kept strictly to myself. My calculations for longitude depended entirely upon the accuracy of my timepiece and with no means of checking the watch I found my mind turning more often than I liked to the possibility of a large error. During the day it was fairly easy to push these fears behind me, but in the night watches, with most of the men asleep, the incubus would not be exorcised. A single minute of error of the watch meant an error of nearly fifteen miles in the distances plotted on the chart. Too far behind would be disappointing, and too far ahead might mean disaster. I had for some days now

kept to the middle latitude of Tobago, and these calculations I
was sure of as the latitude problem has no dependence upon the
time element. I had fearful visions of running between the
islands in the dark, and so on and into the broad Caribbean, with
no hope of beating the boat back against the prevailing wind and
current. These fears became almost a torment towards the last. At
night my ear strained for the sound I dreaded to hear — the deep
diapason of surf breaking upon the shore: and during the day I
searched avidly ahead for land.

Afternoon observations of the sun on the twenty-first day
made the island only forty-six miles ahead. The men seemed
excited and depressed by turn, excepting the five who were now
almost comatose. I folded my chart and put it away in the satchel
without comment, but felt the men's eyes upon me. I dreaded the
moment when I must commit myself by some statement that
could not afford to be wrong.

'When will we see land, sir?' one asked, voicing the question
in all their eyes.

'Tomorrow, I think,' I said.

That night I told the watch on deck to listen carefully for
breakers ahead, and to watch for any sign of broken water or of
land. For my own part, the dark hours seemed interminable and
although sick for lack of sleep I could not rest. As the daylight
came in astern and spread over and ahead, all eyes strained to the
westward, where a faint grey smudge of cloud rested upon the
rim of the sea. But it was not cloud — it was land.

The island swelled imperceptibly in size and colour as we
crept upon it, but at nightfall the boat was still ten miles or more
from shore. The sail was lowered and we lay-to through the dark
hours. I was astonished to find in myself no great elation at the
journey's end: only a feeling of tired content and peace, like a
rocket spent. The men talked the night through, and some
laughter and singing broke out from time to time.

At daylight the island was noticeably nearer, and it was
obvious that the current here set strongly towards the shore. The
blue hills turned to green, and the outlines of trees and palms
emerged gradually from the diluting haze of distance. I pushed
up the tiller and headed the boat towards the northern point of
the island. By noon, the white line of the surf could be seen
fringing the shore as far as the eye could reach and the grim
thunder of the swell hammering upon the beach had a menacing
sound from seaward. As the boat neared the northern point, and
opened the land behind, a marvellous vista of green-topped
palms met our tired eyes, with a foreshore white as snow.

The boat turned the point and steered into the bay, which had
the unreal beauty of a picture from a child's story-book. Quietly,

slowly, wearily the boat moved across the sparkling trans-
parency of the calm water, and at last the stem was resting upon
the white sand.

Big Ju-Ju
A. J. Gilroy

Unfortunately, this is a true story. I wish it wasn't.

Many readers will have been to Africa, and perhaps have a far greater knowledge of African life than I gained whilst stationed in Freetown for a year during the war. I also traded up the coast for a while, and the more I saw of West Africa the less I understood its mysteries. How was it, for example, that whenever anything of international importance happened, whether in Algiers or Natal, the boy who washed my clothes would tell me weeks, sometimes even months, before it was mentioned in the newspapers or on the wireless?

When the great German air-raid on Bizerta took place, I was told by a serious-faced black dhobie-wallah of 'a big disaster up north, many ships sunk, and the water set alight with blazing oil' the very next morning! That news was hushed up by the censor for months.

The incident I am going to write about occurred in 1945. For reasons which will become obvious, I won't give the real name of the ship I was on at the time, nor the real name of anybody I mention. Names might hurt the next-of-kin.

It all started on the outward-bound voyage of the ss *Dalmatian*, a 4,000-ton vessel on which I was serving as third engineer. I had a good Chief, a splendid Second, and the rest of the officers were a good bunch. We left London for Lagos and touched at Freetown, Takoradi and Accra.

Until then the Second Engineer had never been on the Coast and he ridiculed all my stories of mysterious African powers. Since I had many African friends who had told me even more wonderful tales, I took this ridicule very hard, and although he was a great friend of mine, I thought the Second foolish to pooh-pooh my warning to watch his step on the Coast.

After reaching Lagos, we set off for home and, since we were bound for Liverpool, our home port, John (the Second) and I

·were delighted. John had a wife and two children, both the
children being under seven years of age. John himself was 44;
Mrs Mason, his wife, was about 39, and from personal knowledge I knew that they were still very much in love.

On the way home we called in again at Accra, Takoradi, and,
lastly, Freetown, and it is at Freetown that this story begins.

We anchored off King Tom's Wharf, and it wasn't long before
the bum-boats came out to sell us their wares of bananas, pine-
apples and coconuts. The Second and I were standing gazing idly
over the rails, still in dirty boiler suits, when a dug-out canoe
came alongside. It contained two very dark gentlemen and a
good quantity of fruit, and it wasn't very long before John and I
were bartering for bananas.

We eventually agreed on a price — one shilling — for a stalk of
bananas. I selected, as best I could from the deck, the best stalk I
could see, and after hauling it aboard, sent down my shilling in
the little basket attached to the rope for that purpose. John
foolishly put his shilling into the basket as well, before he had
received his bananas, despite my warning not to do so. In consequence, when the bum-boat men sent up a very small and
inferior bunch of bananas, John was very angry and demanded a
far bigger bunch or his money back.

The natives, of course, took no notice of him and began to
make preparations for leaving. Suddenly, John, who was in a
temper such as I had never seen in him before, turned and ran to
Number 4 hatch, upon which lay several old and broken firebars.
Seizing the heaviest firebar there, he ran back to the ship's side,
and even though I struggled to prevent him, threw the firebar
down at the dug-out with all his might.

The two negroes were over the side of the dug-out before the
firebar hit it, for they saw it coming and dived over right away.
Unfortunately, however, the firebar hit the dug-out end on, and
went through the hull like a knife. The dug-out immediately
began to sink, and soon all that remained on the surface was a
little fruit and a bit of dunnage.

Apparently, the negroes had seen my efforts to prevent John
from throwing the bar, for they began to hurl abuse at him but
not at me. John just laughed even when, before they started to
swim away, one negro looked up and shouted: 'All ri', Massa.
You laugh now, but I put ju-ju on you. You never come back to
Freetown again.'

'That won't worry me,' laughed John, and watched them
struggle away to the safety of the shore.

For myself, all I could feel was dismay and, to some extent,
shame at John's terrible revenge on the natives. However, we
sailed from Freetown and there, it seemed, the incident had

ended, though I must confess that I was worried for John's sake about that 'ju-ju'.

We arrived in Liverpool, where John was sent on a fortnight's leave. As I was leaving the ship for another appointment, I deputised for him till he returned. He looked splendidly fit and healthy after his holiday.

The ship was due to leave on the Thursday afternoon tide, bound for Freetown and Lagos again. As I stood on the quayside with Mrs Mason and her two children waving goodbye, I felt an awful coldness steal over me.

The following day, I left for a visit to friends in Rotterdam, and spent a quiet week-end there, but to my surprise, on Monday morning, there arrived a telegram ordering me to report to the Engineer Superintendent in Liverpool as soon as possible. Catching the overnight train in England, I arrived at Head Office on Tuesday morning.

'Sit down, please, Mr Gilroy,' said the Super when I was shown into his office. 'I have sad news for you.'

When I had seated myself, he went on: 'I know you were a great friend of Mr Mason's, so I thought it proper to let you know right away. As you know, I was aboard the *Dalmatian* till she sailed, and John seemed in fine fettle. But on Saturday morning, apparently, he came up off watch at 8am and had a cup of tea. The steward thought he looked all right. But at 8.30, when the steward called him for breakfast, he found him kneeling beside his settee in an attitude of prayer, his head in his clasped hands.

'John had passed away. Heart failure, they think.'

The Superintendent paused.

'I want you to take his place,' he went on after a moment or two. 'Make arrangements with my secretary to fly out, will you? And . . . I'm sorry.'

Stunned by the news, I arranged for my flight and, a fortnight later, stepped aboard the *Dalmatian* in Lagos as second engineer. After I had seen to my gear, I went up to the master's cabin and knocked at the door.

'Come in,' shouted the Captain and, when he saw who I was, he greeted me warmly. 'I'm sorry about John,' he continued when he had poured out the drinks. 'Very bad, leaving a lovely wife and kiddies like that. It's an odd thing, too, but I still can't figure out what was wrong with him. I couldn't put in anywhere for a PM.'

'But I thought it was heart trouble,' I said.

'Well, that just about covers everything,' replied the skipper. 'But I'm blowed if I know what it really was.'

I could have told him, of course. A bunch of bananas and a firebar! And, if anyone wants proof of this story, I have it in my discharge book!

Run Ashore
R. N. Caswell

Whilst other incidents have dimmed, and names of people and places have drifted away on the ebbtide of memory, the recollection of that hundred-yard walk remains etched on my mind and still has the power to bring a shudder of fear.

I had known fear before. After six years of war, naturally I'd known it. Anyone who, in times of stress and danger, says that he has never experienced the emotion of fear is a fool or a liar or both. But this was something far worse than waiting at action stations in the magazine of a warship and hearing the muffled thump, the savage explosion, and feeling the uncontrolled lurch as the vessel heeled under the shock of a torpedo. There was fear then of a different kind; it was the fear that goes hand in hand with exhilaration, when men draw together and, sinking animosities, subdue their individual terror in collective action. The guns were still firing and demanded to be fed. Fear remained, but lurked in the background, sometimes breaking out, masquerading as bravado.

The war had been over in Europe for six months, and three months had elapsed since Hiroshima. The tragedy of Palestine was beginning to unfold — beginning is the wrong word for it had been unfolding for more than a decade, but previously it had been cloaked by more urgent events. At the time, the vessel on which I was serving was engaged on that most odious of duties — immigration control. Most of the time was spent at Haifa, but often sweeps were made in search of those unfortunate wretches who were trying to slip through the net. It was not employment that we relished, for who could enjoy an occupation that entailed striking terror into already bewildered, tragic and homeless women and children. But the powers that be, rightly or wrongly, had so ordered us, and it was always a relief to escape this irksome duty and forget about it for a few days at Alexandria.

In those days, Alex was still a British Fleet base although, even then, the writing was on the wall. The streets were still thronged with a slowly dwindling population of British servicemen whose main topic of conversation was a thing called 'demob'. The Naafi still served at full blast, and the Fleet Club was a going concern. Sister Street, Mohammed Ali Square, and the streets radiating from it like spokes from a hub still catered for the requirements of those same demob-happy sailors, soldiers and airmen. But there was no longer the same need; no longer the same urgency. Death no longer lurked at every shoulder. Alex in wartime had been a haven of forgetfulness, away from the Western Desert and the strife-torn Mediterranean. Alex in peacetime was just another fly-blown Egyptian city from which most people wanted to depart and, having departed, to forget. For those of us, however, who knew that we still had to soldier on for a few years, to whom the word 'demob' was just a newly coined term and to whom home was still a long way off, Alex remained something of a Mecca.

We had been there seven days, and the morrow would see us departing once again for Haifa and those sickening patrols. There was not a soul on board who would not cheerfully have left a breach in the blockage to go steaming to Trieste which, in those days, was a veritable sailors' paradise. The wish being father to the thought, the buzz started in the stokers' heads and swept the ship like wildfire. Trieste it was to be. We hoped.

But Trieste or Haifa, I still had a bill to pay, and if there was a remote chance of our going to Trieste then I would be wise to go ashore and pay it. Who knows, we might even go home from Trieste.

I was the Petty Officer Steward of the Wardroom, and during the vessel's stay in port I had to run up an account for fresh vegetables, fresh fruit, and those bantam eggs — four of them being equivalent to one good egg — with a ships' chandler. It was not a large bill — about twenty to twenty-five pounds in Egyptian currency. I would have preferred that he had come on board for his money but as he hadn't, it meant my going to him. His name was Jim Irish, obviously some corruption of his real name but I never met or heard of anyone who knew his real name. I didn''t much like him, but it was nothing personal. There was nothing racial about it. There were good Wogs and bad Wogs, as there were good and bad Yanks. Jim Irish, in my opinion, was a bit of a shady Wog and it had nothing to do with his colour. I thank the Lord, however, that he must have been held in some respect or fear by his fellow countrymen.

It was evening when I went ashore. I caught the officers' launch. It landed close to number six gate which was where I wished to go. Most of the ships' chandlers were situated on the road leading from it. I forget the name of the road but it is irrelevant. The dress of the day was optional, meaning that one could wear either number tens, or blue trousers with white tropical shirt. I was wearing the latter rig. I wished to transact my business quickly and be away from that none-too-salubrious quarter, for I had promised to meet the PO Sparks and one of the RPOs at the Fleet Club, there to drink warm beer out of sawn-down bottles and play tombola.

A few officers were in the boat and, when we disembarked, they hurried away to catch taxis. I ambled behind slowly, reached the gate and walked up the comparatively wide road to the chandler's. In one trouser pocket I had the money for the account and in the other my own few shekels. Frequently sailors had been knifed and robbed of far less than what I was carrying, so it will be understood that I was averse to lingering, having no wish to finish up in some back-alley with my throat slit. Even now, after the war, these gentry still had a market for paybooks. Mine was slung round my neck on a cord, in compliance with standing orders.

Dusk was gathering — that dusk which heralds the fast-approaching darkness in the Middle East — when I reached the chandler's.

The place was closed. I was annoyed. With all the anger of the inconsiderate young, I hammered at the door. How dare they not be open to await my convenience! Of course, there was no answer. The place was in darkness.

I stood back and looked round. The road was fairly well lighted and down near the dock gate one or two taxis and a few gharries waited. I was about to say 'to hell with Jim Irish' and take a taxi to the Fleet Club, when the boy came up. He had been standing watching me from across the road, a dirty ragged urchin of no more than eight or nine years of age. His once white robe was a filthy grey, and his bare, brown feet looked a matching grey with the dirt that had dried and hardened on them. He tugged at my hand: 'You want Jim Irish, cheef? I take you,' he said.

I shook him off and put my hands in my pockets. In one second flat he would be off with the money I carried; a thin, brown hand, swift as a cobra, would have been inside my pocket and he'd have been away. There would have been nothing I could have done about it, unless I wanted to take on the whole street, relatives and friends, with their cutlery.

He tugged at my shirt: 'I not steal, cheefie. I watch for Jim Irish. I take you.'

'Where is he?' I demanded. He waved a dirty hand, the wide sleeve of his robe slipping, revealing a thin undernourished arm: 'Maybe five minute. You no worry, Cheef. I take you.' He walked away, looking backwards. 'Come. Jim Irish my flend.'

Foolishly, I followed.

He led me across the road and, a little further on, turned into a darkened side street. I hesitated. 'Where are you taking me?' I demanded again. He beckoned: 'Come. No worry.'

I should have left him there and then. What perverseness is there in the human mind? What stupidity is it that makes us go forward when reason and common sense tell us to retreat? Was it something deep in the subconscious that made me put my trust in this child? I shall never know. I do know that in the comparative safety of the road there was not a soul in whom I would have put my trust. Yet I followed the boy.

He was three paces in front of me in that tunnel of a street. As we progressed the gloom deepened into darkness. What little light remained in the sky could not penetrate here. It was dark ahead; it was dark behind. I heard naked feet pattering close. I felt ghostly bodies glide up to me, and touch me with long, claw-like hands, and then flit past. From ghastly tumbledown hovels came hissing whispers: 'Cheef. Cheef.' 'Inside cheef.' 'You wanch nice girl, ten yera. Verra calean.' 'Blue pictures, cheef.' I felt fear but, so far, not unreasoning fear. I knew that to have turned and run back to the safety of the road we had just left would have ensured that I would not last half a dozen steps. I had not been molested and now, not far ahead, I could see the flickering lights of a parallel road.

The lights, for me, were just a mirage, for a little more than half-way along the boy turned abruptly left. 'Where are you taking me?' I asked again, this time not demanding, only fearfully pleading. He turned his head, his teeth gleaming in what, to me, was an evil smile, his hand beckoning, waving me on.

My eyes had now become accustomed to the darkness and in the awful gloom I could see. What I saw was not reassuring to my now almost panicking mind. Surely this could not be a place where human beings dwelt? It was even narrower than the street we had turned from. No more than twelve feet in width, it was just dusty hard-baked mud for a slit of a road without pavements, between broken-down, decaying houses that had holes for doors and windows. Refuse was littered everywhere in great heaps, and the stench of rotting food vied with the foul smell of excrement. The sky above was a dark grey pencil line, and ahead not a glimmer of light showed a goal of any kind. In doorways lurked filthy, ragged men, women and children; lean, hungry, vengeful faces leered and scowled; and dark eyes looked at me with unblinking, sullen hatred as though I were personally responsible for all the squalor and misery of their environment. The whole place, the very people themselves, stank of evil. And

God knows, what else could be radiated from such degradation and from such dregs of humanity?

I felt trapped. I dared not go back and I was afraid to go forward; and yet could not, would not for all the devils in creation, stand rooted there. With thumping heart, and on jellied legs, I walked after my diminutive guide. He was now eight or ten paces ahead.

Again came those awful sibilant whispers, like the hissing of snakes; again the pattering feet, a nerve-racking sound that made my flesh creep and caused me to jerk my head from side to side with quick frightened movements. And then, dear Christ, a whole bunch of those spectre-like skeletons moved menacingly towards me, detaching themselves from their hovels and silently creeping up behind and beside me, forming a crescent of jostling bodies. And from all around came that obscene hissing of 'Cheef, Cheef, Cheef.'

Did I imagine it, or did I catch the glint of a knife-blade in one of the many hands that reached out for me? I could almost feel it prodding, pricking and entering my flesh and twisting between my ribs. I must have sobbed, or called out, or made some kind of noise, for there was my infant guide standing in front of me, angrily waving them away and cursing them in Egyptian. Three times I heard 'Jim Irish!' spoken shrilly by those young lips. There was a lessening of the pressure around me; the hands dropped from me. With blessed relief I became aware that they were moving away from me, although they still hovered close, contenting themselves with that hissing sound and occasionally darting at me. Others who came from ahead were waved away, or melted into doorways at the sound of my guide's voice saying over and over again: 'Jim Irish! Jim Irish!'

I had more of a grip on myself as we walked the remaining distance of that horrifying hundred yards, but I was still in a state of abject terror. Hurrying, but desperately trying not to break into a run, we reached the end of the street, with the creatures following close behind.

A short walk took us across a small square. The strident notes of Egyptian music from the cafés and the shrieking of female singers, which normally set my teeth on edge, sounded like a rendering of 'The Messiah'.

Jim Irish was seated in a native café. I must have been still visibly shaking, for he ordered brandy for me without asking, and continued to do so for the next half-hour. I willingly let him pay, and gave all the loose change I had to a ragged but delighted urchin. He ran off shouting gleefully, never having known, legally, so much wealth as twenty piastres.

I never discovered, and indeed did not care, what hold Jim

Irish had over those people of that little underworld, but he must
have been the big boss of some racket or other for them to forgo
their easy pickings at the mere mention of his name.

The short rest, plus the effects of the brandy, had brought me
back to a state of normalcy and I began to think of my appointment at the Fleet Club. I fingered the pulpy notes in my pocket.
'Come on,' I said arrogantly, 'let's get this bill fixed!'

Jim Irish stood up. 'All right,' he answered, 'we go back to
shop. Only a few minute. We take short cut!'

And that is exactly what we did.

Almost a quarter of a century has elapsed since I last visited
Alexandria. I called there a few times more in a warship, but
have never visited the port in a merchant vessel. On the few
occasions when I did visit with the Royal Navy, I insisted that
Jim Irish come on board for his money. Not for the life of me
would I ever take it ashore again. Although, full of brandy, I had
made the return journey in his company, I would not take the
chance of a repetition of that hundred yards of short cut with an
infant for a guide.

Sometimes, in reminiscence, I wonder what became of my
ragged urchin. Maybe he is now the Jim Irish of that little underworld. I will never know. I do know, however, that but for him I
should never have survived in that hideous street. Conversely I
also know that but for him I should never have ventured near the
place.

Today and Yesterday
John Moody

Anybody over fifty can recall a time when children were pleasant and football was a sport instead of a blood bath.

Great changes have taken place. Changes that usually take a hundred years or more have happened in thirty years. The dividing line was the Second World War. Those who managed to survive it may well have more difficulty coping with the peace of today.

Life at sea has not escaped the general upheaval. It is fair to say that the Nelsonic outlook had prevailed almost unscathed up to the outbreak of the last war. It is true that flogging and keel-hauling had been abolished (with regrets in some quarters), but there was always a lurking suspicion that any signs of softness or concessions to comfort would mean the end of seafaring. The open bridge was still in vogue, with the helmsman exposed to the elements, the theory being that enclosed he would probably fall asleep at the wheel.

The big breakthrough came when the Americans launched their massive Liberty shipbuilding programme during the war, one of the deciding factors in winning the war. These ships were considered to have more than paid their way if they managed to complete only one voyage, but the standards of comfort on board were higher than anything seen before the war — and the war was still on!

I well remember a voyage on a hardcase tramp. At the outset, after signing on, the firemen took one look below and trooped ashore. They informed the police at the dock gates that they were deserting and wished to be put in jail. The police said it would mean three months in the clink, to which they readily agreed. Apparently the replacements had just come out of jail for they were put aboard by police who waited at the foot of the gangway until we sailed.

Life was never dull on that ship. Soon after sailing one of the firemen decided to throw his weight about with the donkeyman. The latter did not hesitate. He dropped the fireman cold on the engine-room plates with one blow from a shifting spanner. From then on the donkeyman was greatly respected by all and was never bothered again. Weakness was fatal. From the start it was essential to show who was in charge. Bucko-mates did not disappear with sail. At times they had to know how to handle themselves on tramp ships as well.

Coal-firing firemen were a race apart — long since extinct. I suspect that many of them are still feeding furnaces below. It used to be said that their sole gear on joining ship was a pack of cards and a sweat rag, and this was not far from the truth. Often they had no more than the clothes they stood up in. Our lot on that particular ship were no exception. They would sally forth ashore in the same rig, regardless of whether the temperature was 10 below or 110 in the shade. They were quite impervious to cold or heat and scared of nobody. Invariably our crowd were brought back by the local gendarmes, battered and bruised but in no way mollified. Come the night they would set off for a return bout.

At sea nobody could better them for keeping steam. Even in the deadly heat of the Red Sea they stuck it out when lesser breeds, even though accustomed to hot climates, collapsed on the stokehold plates. They were a hard tough breed who did an unpleasant exacting job well, but there is no place for them in today's automated ships. Now it is technique, not muscle and guts, that counts.

We had a fourteen-day ice-box situated on the lower bridge. The old hands could tell to the day when the ice would melt and the meat inside go rotten. After that it was salt-beef, salt-pork, and dried fish, none of it particularly appetising, although I understand that such provisions were expensive. The salt-pork was always served with mustard pickles, which helped some-what to get it down. The chief steward broke out the lime-juice when the fresh provisions were finished, usually to muttered accusations of adulteration. At least it was interesting to find out at first-hand why the British were called Limeys.

Our Old Man so enjoyed the cook's dried fish cakes that he was prone to ask for them in restaurants ashore, and appalled when told that they did not serve rotting cod to their customers. Curry appeared every morning for breakfast. It varied a lot in contents and smell. When it was particularly obnoxious and nobody dare touch it, the Old Man would delight in having two helpings. Then he would leave the saloon and bring the lot up in his toilet. The message was that if he could eat it so could we. Thursdays and Sundays were gala days. On those occasions we had an egg for breakfast and duff for lunch. Duff was a dessert, and a cook's reputation was made (or lost) on the duff he made. Sometimes it was very good and filling, which was most important.

A tin of condensed milk was supposed to last each man three weeks. A well-known lady Member of Parliament denied in the House that this was insufficient, for she herself had experimented and found it adequate. Needless to say she was hardly the number one pin-up aboard ships. Much ingenuity was shown in preserving the precious tin from the ravages of cockroaches and other marauding insects. Usually this consisted of suspending the tin from the deckhead underneath another can containing water, in the hope that the little beasts would meet a watery grave.

The cook lived in a permanent state of siege. His galley was just aft of number three hatch and had the usual stable-type doors. The lower half was kept firmly bolted and a cleaver kept handy to repel all disgruntled invaders. Often enough the mess-kits came flying back at him through the open top half. His was a most unenviable job, for he had little enough to cook with and tried valiantly to ring the changes on dried vegetables and salt meat. When the potatoes ran out yams became the substitute as often as not, and there is not much you can concoct out of yams.

Outside the galley was a hand-pump. When the water was running low this was kept locked with a massive chain and padlock. If the chain rattled the cook would appear at the galley half-door with the cleaver poised ominously. At certain times we lined up with a bucket and pumped the bucket half full. This had to suffice for washing and dhobeying, but spotless whites were hardly the rig of the day.

In port the lighting went off at 5 pm. This was an economy to save the donkeyman's overtime. After tea there would be a mad rush to get shaved, washed and dressed before the blackout and usually one was caught about half way. We all had oil lamps with a single wick but the mate, being a man of some position, had two wicks. We then queued up in his cabin to tie our ties and comb our hair before the exodus to the shore. The mate also possessed a small portable electric fan — the envy of everybody as it was the only one on board. He would solemnly take this into the saloon and position it to waft a cooling breeze on himself. One considered oneself very fortunate to sit even on the fringes of this sybaritic luxury.

Money was in short supply but somehow it seemed to stretch quite a long way, because then the pound sterling had real value, whereas today it is only play-money and worthless. One could have a great night out in Japan on a pound; today there is no change out of forty.

Life at sea ran along well-established lines. Deck officers never contemplated marriage until they had obtained their master's certificate, and then stayed at sea waiting for the eventual goal — command. It did not always happen. Junior engineers swotted for their certificates in order to reap the bonanza of becoming chief engineer, but many never got past second engineer. For top jobs you waited to step into dead men's shoes. In the crowded grim fo'cs'le, some sailors studied to become mates — determined to get out of it. The carrot offered was a rigid step by step improvement in conditions as one slowly climbed the ladder. This has largely disappeared, replaced by a rather confusing and contradictory system of sameness for all, irrespective of position or effort. In the old days, of course, people could be sacked and were sacked. Most realised the reality of this and made sure that it did not happen to them. Others were waiting for your job if you lost it.

In consequence of all this standards were high and there was a lot of professional pride in a job well done. The shipowner, whether good or bad, was known. He was a real person and often visited his ships in a home port. This tended to create a feeling of personal identity. Today in many cases it is very difficult to find just who you are working for. Tax-dodging practices worked out by clever accountants can generate a very cynical response from those who work for those responsible. On the whole, going to sea before the war was a career which was considered a well-worthwhile one. The paradox today is that great advances in material and monetary conditions have not brought a relative feeling of satisfaction and contentment.

Unfortunately, today life at sea is often considered a temporary business for getting some ready cash together. It is human nature, I suppose, never to be completely satisfied with one's lot, but it seems too common a malaise everywhere today.

When sail gave way to steam there were many who derided it and swore that seafaring as they knew it was finished. Now, the conventional ship with character is surrendering in its turn to the boxes of today. But no doubt a new generation of seamen will find that the super-tanker, the bulk-carrier, the container ship and the roll-on roll-off vessel also have a soul.

Archangel for Orders
A. Collinge

I met Johnny and Bill in the mission, and we went across to the Mercantile Marine Office to see what jobs were going. The desk department official pulled our cards out and grunted: 'Three AB's. There's jobs on the *Kyloe* and the *Woodham Rover*.'

'Where are they bound?'

'The *Kyloe* is loading coal for Spain, and the *Woodham Rover* is going light-ship to Archangel for timber.'

Bill spoke from behind his pipe. 'Let's go to Russia for a lark!'

So we went to Russia.

There are three reasons why I remember that trip more than most: it was my first trip to the USSR; I was in hospital there; and then there was the number of rats we cleared off the ship.

She was lying down at Irlam Wharf discharging sulphur. She was an old ship and rumour had it that she had been on the bottom twice — once in Bari, Italy, when the big explosion happened there during the war. She turned out to be a very good sea ship, but that was as far as her good points went.

Before we left the sulphur wharf, the Port Health Authority collected over eighty rats just lying in the tween decks and on the beams. On the way to Archangel we collected 285 more of all shapes, sizes and colours, as we cleaned the holds out of their past cargoes of sulphur and coal. Bill was the only AB on day-work, so the watches as well worked overtime during the ten-day run. The holds were filthy and strewn with dunnage. We had to work with damp kerchiefs over our mouths, but still the mixture of sulphur and coal-dust clogged our throats and nostrils.

Dead rats appeared everywhere, and we kept a tally of them as we shovelled them into sack after sack. To bath ourselves, we had to get our water from the pump amidships, hump it aft, and do the bucket drill. After a few days my skin broke out into a rash, mainly round the groin where my dungarees chafed the soft flesh.

It was a pleasant trip through the Minch and north about the Shetlands to Lofoten, and it continued calm, though cold, as we rounded North Cape. Since it was the end of September we saw very little of the aurora borealis, though its waning light could sometimes be seen in the night watches.

In the White Sea we picked up the Russian pilot who took us up the Dvina River to Archangel. The customs came aboard and searched us thoroughly in the early hours of the morning. Everyone was mustered amidships during the cold, bleak middle watch and cameras, binoculars and film were put under bond. Literature that was considered decidedly capitalistic was confiscated. The chief customs official was wearing an American Navy waterproof pea-jacket and I asked him where he had got it. He said he got it while serving with the US Navy.

In the morning light a hefty, ruddy-faced girl dragged our stern line to a bollard. There were plenty of men on the jetty but no-one ventured to give her a hand.

The Dvina is a wide river and the country is flat, with little scenic beauty. There were two other British ships in, the *Thistleford* and the *Coulbreck*, besides a couple of Scandinavians. It appeared that we were the fourth British ship to touch Archangel after the post-war Anglo-Soviet trade agreement. This apparently specified that British ships should go out empty to load timber while Russian ships went to Britain empty to load agricultural machinery.

Armed guards with green caps were placed on the wharf. Approximately a third of the ship's crew was issued with passes to go ashore and warned not to forget the midnight curfew. Johnny got a pass. Bill and I didn't — because our photographs were not properly fixed in our discharge-books, or so they said. I chased the steward up to get a doctor on board. The steward was a Bombay Christian and gave me a sermon on morals, since he jumped to conclusions about my skin complaint, and for the rest of the trip he was very concerned about my making my peace with God.

A woman doctor came aboard with the agent a few days later. I stripped and she inspected my body with professional unconcern, saying that I'd better go to the clinic to have a blood-test — just in case. I explained to her through the agent-interpreter that I couldn't get a pass to go ashore. She immediately told the agent to get me one, and said that she should have seen me as soon as we docked. He waved his hands despairingly and said the police issued passes, not he.

Bill, Johnny and I were standing on the poop during the dinner hour. There were some children playing on the wharf, so Bill fetched some chocolate and threw it down to them. Johnny and I did the same. They grinned their thanks at us but their pleasure was short-lived for one of the green-caps hurried along, took the chocolate from the children, unslung his rifle and pointed it at us. We called him all the names under the nautical sun, but he only scowled and snapped the safety-bolt of his rifle back. Bill was fuming. 'The lousy bastard,' he said. Johnny nudged me and mimicked him: 'Let's go to Russia for a lark!'

The pass came aboard in the early afternoon and the agent took me ashore in a Moscow-built car. When we arrived at the clinic, he ushered me inside, with no waiting, to the doctor, a big blonde woman. There were four girl students in the clinic as well, all about twenty years of age, and they looked on with keen interest and feminine giggles while the doctor made her inspection. She spoke to the agent who interpreted that it looked just like a severe inflammation caused by the rough chafing of my dungarees but that she would take a blood-test to make sure.

From there we went to the general hospital and another woman doctor. She was a tall, serene, kindly-looking woman and this time I had to strip completely so that she could inspect my skin all over. A prescription was made up and I was told to report back in two days' time. The agent took me down to the ferry this time and, telling me which ship to get off at, left me to my own devices.

A cold, biting wind swept the river as the ferry steamed under way. It was fairly crowded, mainly with women dressed in clean but shabby clothes six years behind the fashions.

I got off at the wrong jetty, though I could see the ship ahead of me. Between the ship and me lay a long, wide creek, jammed up with a log-boom. Wondering how to get across before darkness fell, I noticed a boy running across the logs. It seemed easy and, when he came ashore, I offered him some cigarettes to show me the knack of log-hopping. He quickly stowed them in his pocket, gesticulated to me to keep to the outside of the log-boom, then threw a plank across the mud on to the nearest log so that I could get a running start.

I followed his advice and kept up a quick, trotting pace until one of the logs of the boom chain sank beneath me, leaving me precariously balanced, submerged to the knees in freezing cold water. Having an overcoat on, and not wishing to go swimming at that time of year, I scrambled as best I could on to the next log without taking a tumble and reached the far shore and the ship without further mishap.

My skin rash broke out more severely than ever the following day and I went back to the general hospital. My blood-test proved negative-negative, and I was immediately packed off to another hospital along with Ahmed, an old Arab fireman suffering from stomach ulcers. This hospital was just outside the town and both of us were in there for eight days. Three times a day, nurses came to anoint my body with ointment and every mid-day a youngish, cheery woman doctor came to give me an injection in the arm. It was an injection that made me feel as though my head was going to blow off.

The stately, serene doctor came to inspect me every second day and, through the agent, she asked me what drugs and health-restoring equipment were being used in England. Not being a medical man, I couldn't tell her much, but she seemed interested in what little I did know.

I had a small ward to myself and received a continuous stream of curious visitors from the other wards. The bosun and Johnny came to see me and brought me some chocolate and cigarettes as well as the embroidery I did in my spare time.

One girl, aged about seventeen, came into my ward regularly. She had had an eye removed and the socket was bandaged securely. She was a dark, pleasant-looking girl called Tamara. An old woman generally accompanied her and I offered the girl some chocolate which she refused though I could see that she wanted it. I gave it to the old woman instead. She chuckled and stuffed it in the girl's pocket as though to say: 'I'm not scared of people seeing me take luxuries. I'm too old to care.'

There was only one patient who could speak fluent English, and he was an ageing Russian sailor who before the war years had lived in San Francisco. He used to reminisce over those days as we played dominoes together.

The food was good and, though all the meat I was served was goat meat, I enjoyed it. All the time I was in hospital I came across only one male doctor, the radiographer. Every day I had a walk in the hospital grounds with Tamara and a couple of her friends, watching the life on the river and the Spitfires soaring overhead.

My skin rash was still traceable eight days after my admission but both Ahmed and I were chased out of hospital and back to the ship because the ship was due to sail over the weekend. She had shifted berth so, naturally, when we got down to the wharf, our passes were in the care of a green-cap higher up the river and we couldn't get aboard. The agent went hot foot round and round questioning the impassive guards and, after three-quarters of an hour, the passes turned up.

The mate asked me to turn to straight away and, believe it or not, the job was working cargo. Johnny and Bill had already been winch-driving that morning with the bosun as hatchman, and they had had to work Nos 1 and 2 hatches, switching from winch to winch. I took over with Wally, another AB, and we relieved Bill and Johnny.

Of course, the complaints started. We all saw the Captain and asked him what the idea was, having to do the Russians' cargo work for them. He said they couldn't get any winch-drivers, and Bill replied: 'They've had them all week. What's the matter today? And, anyhow, one man shouldn't have to work two winches.' The Old Man was decidedly worried. 'The Russians have been working two winches,' he said, 'so can you.' Bill flared up. 'I'm not a Russian. They might do in Rome what the Romans do, but there's a British flag flying over this ship.' The Captain fell back on the final argument: 'Do the job or get logged.' It wasn't worth getting logged for, so the job went on, everyone being in a black mood.

As it was our last night in Archangel, Johnny and I and a few of the lads went to the International Club. We went into a big hall when we arrived, expecting a concert. Instead, we had our ears bashed for a solid hour by a Party member who was pep-talking the younger generation of Archangel on the finer points of Communism. Fortunately, we couldn't understand Russian.

Johnny and I sidled out when the orator was reaching a crescendo and found a bar. A glass of beer cost 7s. 6d., and vodka 6s. There was a small dance-hall where the local English-speaking girls, in between games and dancing, gave us private lectures on the evils of Western capitalism, so Johnny and I moved over to the larger hall where the girls couldn't speak English and smiled at you every time you trod on their toes.

We ended up back among the linguists at closing time, arguing the pros and cons of East and West and, as the East didn't like some of the home-truths from the West, a bitter argument was averted only when the bosun started us all singing the *Internationale*, though his words didn't sound like the usual ones. Come to think of it, the bosun had talked his way into a shore pass by saying he was a big-shot Party man from Manchester, along with Harry Pollitt.

The following day we left after another thorough search by the Customs who seemed to be worried about people getting out of the country.

After clearing the White Sea, we ran into some real winter weather straight from the North Pole. We edged into the Norwegian fjords at North Cape, buffeted and blown by a force ten, and frozen with icy rain and sleet. We picked up a couple of Norsk pilots and missed a lot of the bad weather on the inside route to Narvik. The fjords are grim in October, but beautiful and grand to see, with the mountainous scenery covered with an early snowfall.

As the deck-boy and an ordinary-seaman were in my watch during the two days when we had pilots aboard, the Old Man had me doing four-hour tricks at the helm. It was a good job the ship steered well.

Eventually we reached Cardiff, paid off and, with a sigh of relief, trained north to Manchester. We vowed 'no more Russia for us,' and laughed. However, we laughed too soon, as our next ship went to Odessa.

Midnight Prowler
Jim Petrie

Strange chaps are some shipmates.

We were homeward bound to Rotterdam and the United Kingdom after a long voyage trading in the Pacific Ocean and the China Sea when the Chief came to see me. Paddy Riley, he said, was behaving oddly. A middle-aged seafarer of tough Liverpool-Irish origins, Paddy Riley seemed to be suffering from insomnia and hallucinations. Several night-watch crew had seen him prowling about the deck and alleyways, mostly in the officers' accommodation in the middle watch. He appeared doped, dizzy and oddly elated, but he was unable to talk with any degree of coherence.

I decided to see Paddy Riley privately. He was in a very nervous state and his hands shook. First he locked his fingers together, then he unlocked them. Then he put one hand behind his head and down the back of his neck, and then tried the other hand. I tried him with a tot of rum and he took it in a gulp. His eyes rolled in their sockets and the lids went up and down several times. At last the tears came and he approached normality.

In Tanjong Priok, in Java, he told me eventually, he had gone ashore to a well-known dance-hall and wine bar. The local people had proved more than friendly and Paddy drank more than was good for him. In the end, he passed out, though fortunately in excellent company. One of the local families, having failed to locate his ship, took him home, planning no doubt to make another attempt when Paddy sobered up.

As befitted a seaman, Paddy woke up first, much the worse for wear, and found he had been sleeping on the floor of a wooden house. Around him slept four nubile young ladies, daughters of the house. In the shadows there might even have been other relatives — no doubt there were — but Paddy was in no state to put two and two together. Garbled stories of abducted seamen ran through his head and, quickly checking that nothing was missing, he gathered his clothes together and ran away. He found his ship without difficulty, for he had not been far from the waterfront, but several members of the crew saw him come aboard in his bare feet and without his shirt and jacket on. After the ship had sailed he had found that something was missing after all — his seaman's identity card with his name and address and details of his family.

Having told his story — or what he could remember of it — Paddy had become the target for all kinds of shipboard wit. At first he had enjoyed the notoriety. But then someone, who was a near neighbour in Liverpool, had suggested that Bridget, Paddy's wife, would be interested to learn of Paddy's escapade, and that she would be still more interested if some eighteen-year-old Javanese beauty came looking in Liverpool for her Irish lover.

The sad fact was that Paddy Riley — one of the original Liverpool firemen and as hard as nails — was terrified of his fifteen-stone wife. He had more than once been heavily punished with her rolling-pin for coming home drunk. The thought of what would happen if a Javanese girl armed with his identity card came seeking him at home unnerved him completely. He could not sleep at night unless he had a few drinks.

Of course, his beer ration did not extend far enough to allow him a sound sleep every night, and so he began to try and ingratiate himself with others in the hope of being given an extra can or two. But this did not work for long, and indeed, after a few days, it had led to his ostracism. No-one wanted anything to do with him.

In a worse mess than ever, Paddy hit upon what seemed a bright idea. In Singapore many of those on board had bought a cheap after-shave lotion which was nothing but perfumed alcohol of a particularly rough kind. Some of the officers, in particular, had acquired good stocks of it.

It was after-shave lotion that Paddy was seeking on his midnight prowls, and it was drinking the stuff that had reduced him to the state he was in.

Having diagnosed his ills I did my best to cure them. A seaman's life being what it is, I never did discover how he enjoyed his homecoming, but I am sure his dusky — and innocent — beauties never bothered him in Scotland Road.

The Advantages of Seafaring
Ken Hardman

To be frank, the average modern seaman does not go to sea because he likes the feel of the blown spume against his face. Nor does he, Masefield-like, revel in the ever-changing moods of the element on which he sails. I doubt if anyone — a comparative handful of dedicated poets and storm-lovers apart — has ever liked being on the sea (as distinct from being on dry land looking at the sea) in its more violent moods. That indefinable call of the sea can and does draw hundreds of young men to the training colleges and, ultimately, to the sea itself, but it cannot hold them there once the initial romance and adventure has worn a trifle thin. Many of them retire, disillusioned, after a few years, and slide back into a shore job as gracefully as possible.

To the not inconsiderable remainder, on the other hand, the manifold advantages of a seafaring life — that unique combination of gaiety and boredom, peace and frustration, beauty and sordidness — become more and more apparent as the years go by, until they reach the stage where they begin to wonder how the devil people manage to live permanently ashore at all.

This realisation is gradual and made up of small things. At home, on leave, you notice how so-and-so, who used to sit next to you at school, has aged so obviously that he might be taken for your uncle. An isolated case, you think. The other schoolmates and contemporaries pop up, and you see the beginnings of a sedentary paunch here and a factory or machine-shop pallor there. All this, of course, is pure personal vanity; but it is a vanity which everyone possesses in some degree. No-one likes to appear to grow old — and it is my steadfast opinion that, as a general rule, seamen retain their youth, both physically and mentally, far longer than their shorebound contemporaries. I don't really know why; perhaps there's something in that sea-air stuff after all.

Another aspect of the personal vanity view, which might be

neither readily admitted nor discussed but which is nevertheless still there, is this: the very fact that one is a seaman, even in these days of package tours, leads others to recognise that one is a 'man of the world', a man who has been places and seen things. An adroitly handled phrase, like 'When I passed through Panama a month ago', can still reduce a non-seagoing gathering to something akin to awe. A man who can speak of a city at the other end of the world with the easy familiarity with which his friends speak of the neighbouring market town is definitely not a person to argue with about world affairs. In the street and in the pub the seaman's friends greet him with that strange mixture of interest and envy that so often marks the landsman's approach to anyone connected with the sea and ships. They listen quietly to his stories and confide in him that if it hadn't been for this or that they too would have gone to sea.

But these are somewhat nebulous things. The down to earth advantages of a professional sailor's lot are, to a professional sailor, so numerous that it is difficult to know where to begin.

I suppose that, in this mercenary world, the question of money must take first place. Here, a seafarer has a unique advantage over a shore wage-earner in that he is practically forced to save a substantial part of his earnings — simply because there is little or no opportunity to spend money at sea. For much of the year there are none of the expensive diversions of life ashore to worry him. Nor is this too much of a hardship, for everyone aboard is, literally and metaphorically, in the same boat. Whilst the landsman decides to stop off at the local for a few beers, or to take his girl friend to a show, the sailor in the middle of the Atlantic blithely and inexpensively plays cribbage, smokes his duty-free cigarettes, drinks his excise-free beer, yarns with his mates, and turns in.

There are, of course, the 'subs' or advances on wages drawn in foreign ports, but these are seldom large, and the Old Man or the company is likely to ensure that there are not too many of them. The result is quite a substantial pay-off in the home port, augmented if he is lucky by overtime. Jack, when he comes ashore at home, can usually afford to live like a king, at least for the length of his leave — in fact, the rate at which some seamen spend money over a brief time might even make a king blanch. There is nothing quite like the good spirits and downright jubilation — known somewhat cynically as the 'Channels' — of a homeward-bound crew with the hard-earned pay-off looming large on the horizon. Whatever trials and tribulations the trip has had to offer, you suddenly feel that it was worth it after all.

The last generation's criticism of life at sea — poor and even bad conditions — is scarcely valid any longer. Admittedly there are still a few of the older ships, mostly under foreign flags, where the living accommodation leaves something to be desired, but these can't last much longer. Nor will they be the subject of my sentimental tears when they do finally end up at the breakers. Almost all the new ships now being built have excellent quarters for every member of the crew. Food and victualling, whilst varying greatly from ship to ship and from company to company, is more than fair on the whole, and most people eat better at sea than they do at home. The days of skimping and saving on ships' catering bills are the days of yesteryear.

Many years ago a certain lady politician is said to have made the statement that seamen should not require payment for their work. The joys of travel, she maintained, should be sufficient in themselves. After all, her friends paid hundreds of pounds in passage money to go to exactly those places to which the seaman went free. There was an obvious flaw in her logic; but, nevertheless, the so-called 'wanderlust' has always been a powerful trait in most men. Even the most entrenched bank-clerk or civil servant must dream at times of visiting 'far away places with strange sounding names', as a popular song once put it. Whilst there are few romantic illusions left for the seasoned sailor — he soon discovers that places and people are much the same the world over — the old thrill of new horizons does not completely desert him. Though he may suspect that Zanzibar will turn out to be the usual conglomeration of flies, heat and stenches, he still watches it grow out of the Indian Ocean with interest. There is always the sense of 'going places' about a ship and the very thought of exchanging it for an immovable office or factory is enough to send a shudder through the nautical frame.

How well married life mixes with the sea is always a debatable subject. To the sailor, homecoming is the essence of a voyage, a distilled pleasure that never palls in a lifetime at sea. Why go away at all then, if there is so much pleasure in the home?

So much depends upon the individuals concerned that no hard and fast rule can be laid down. Many men leave the sea when they marry: some through wifely pressure, others because of a natural inclination to be with their family as much as possible. But many also stay at sea, and are apparently quite happy about it. I read an article in an illustrated magazine recently: the magazine had conducted a survey among wives in three classes, or income groups, to discover what job or profession was most conducive to a happy married life in each group. It was the usual hackneyed kind of thing, but the unusual point about it was that, in two of the classes, seamen romped home hands down.

The wives concerned gave their reasons — and quite substantial ones they were too. One said that every time her
husband came home it was like a second honeymoon. Another
maintained that in nautical marriages there was never time for
the couple to get tired of each other: they always tried to look
their best and be on their best behaviour to each other during the
husband's leaves, all of which it would be well-nigh impossible
to keep up indefinitely. All things considered, I believe a seaman
can have a happy married life provided that he confines himself
to comparatively short trips. Even the most amenable wives are
likely to baulk at the two-year trips which were common at one
time.

Every seafarer, no doubt, dreams of a last homecoming: his
wife jubilant because he is home to stay, his friends smilingly
helpful about finding a job for him. . . . But, should it happen,
there will be a certain condescension in the manner of these
friends. He will be moving into their everyday world of office
and factory, and no longer of particular interest to them; indeed,
the anchor-swallowing seafarer must begin shore life near the
foot of the ladder that they have long since climbed, so it will
seem that he is a pretty ordinary fellow after all.

As the months go by he will see his shore-life begin to settle
into the rut of mediocrity. He will go to work each morning and
return home each night, and his wife, unable to maintain the
desperate gaiety of a brief leave, will lapse into being a normal
housewife. Money will be scarce, and the seafarer will find that
he has to make small, annoying economies: he could get a
hundred cigarettes at sea for the price he now pays for twenty,
and the long, money-saving weeks afloat are impossible to
imitate among the tempting shops and pubs. He will grow
moody as the prospect of an infinity of grey days weighs down
on him like a solid thing. 'But others do it', his wife may argue.
Yes, others do it. But they have not been to sea; they have not
been hopelessly prejudiced by a life that teaches men to take
their pleasures in short, intense interludes.

And all at once the choice will be there, the choice that faced
John Winter in the poem by Laurence Binyon, when he crept
from his wife's side at dead of night and breathed 'a breath more
free' as he made his way once more to the docks. Does one want a
life that flows on with the grey sameness of an inland river, or a
life that floods and ebbs like the tides of the sea?

There are contrasts, of course, in the life of a sailor. Where else
on the face of God's earth can one meet with such violent contrasts as those which occur in the length of a single voyage? In a
matter of days the weather can change from freezing cold to
searing heat. Jerseys and heavy clothes are abandoned like

useless husks and a man steps forth in the near-forgotten boyish freedom of shorts, feeling the sweat channel down the browning skin of his bare chest. Now he curses the heat as a few days before he cursed the cold, for it is always vitally necessary to curse something. But the cursing goes no deeper than the mouth, no deeper than the delicately traced patterns of flying fish on the empty blue-silk sea.

And then there is the contrast in scene. For days on end the ship steams peaceful and alone, the men buried in the monotony of routine. Watch follows watch, starlit lookout follows thoughtful wheel, until the very soul is drugged and calm as a sunlit pool and a man might be content to sail on thus for ever, divorced and apart from the troubles of the world.

But suddenly this quiet world explodes into the bustle of ports and harbours; the ship is invaded by screaming hordes of cargo-workers and businessmen; black, brown, yellow and olive faces crowd around him in splendid confusion, entreating him to buy this or that, to visit the Casablanca bar just up the street where English is spoken, or the El Ranchito Bordello on the outskirts of town where the girls are very nice. At once he is fully alive again, awakening refreshed to the sights and sounds of a strange land.

It is now that the door of another watertight compartment in his life opens. The port lies on the doorstep before him in the soaring splendour of tall buildings or the pathetic squalor of clustered huts. For a few hours, a few days, it is his to do with as he chooses; he may drink its wine and savour its women, he may walk its tree-lined streets or twisting dirt tracks, or he may simply stand at the ship's rail and gaze across the waters of the harbour, content to know that he is here in a foreign land which is but a name in an atlas to most of his friends at home.

And all the time the work of the ship goes on: cargo swings ashore in bales and boxes, the end of the line for an export drive which began in London and Sheffield and Glasgow. There are wires to drag and splice, blocks to rig, hatches to open, meals to cook, boilers to tend; all the thousand jobs that keep a working ship alive and well must be attended to, though the sailor's head may throb from a wild night ashore and the heat of the sun hits his sweating back like a blow. But there is always tonight to live for, tonight and a host of other golden nights stretching away into the future like a bright string of fairy lights.

Since time immemorial the sea has been regarded as a moulder of character. Family black sheep, erring sons, and just plain ruffians, were pushed off to sea as a last resort, the theory apparently being that the sea was an almighty leveller of men, and that they would return home chastened, wiser and better beings. Nowadays the practice is not as popular as it was, but the

fact remains that a few years at sea can do wonders for a lad if he
has half a mind to avail himself of the unique advantages it offers
in the way of self-education. I don't mean education in the
scholastic sense — although that is easy to come by, too — but in
the wider sense of the word: a breadth of mind that comes only
with meeting and mingling with people of many races, under-
standing to the best of your ability their ways of life and view-
points; and, above all, learning to tolerate that which you cannot
agree with nor understand. I have sailed in the fo'c'sles of ships
with learned men who never saw the inside of more than a
primary school, but they could leave the majority of university
graduates standing in their grasp of life and its implications.

So rests the case for the sea. Doubtless just as many arguments
could be made against the sea as a livelihood. I could find a few
myself. It is, as all things are, a matter of personal taste; either
you like it or you don't. For myself, I can make no stronger
statement than this: if I had a son and he showed the slightest
inclination towards a nautical life, he would go away to sea with
my blessing.

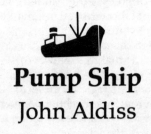

Pump Ship
John Aldiss

'When I get out of the Navy,' a young Doc once said to me, 'I intend to specialise in surgical plumbing. Do you realise that you probably pump ship two thousand times in one year, and in a lifetime of three score and ten you have 140,000 pump ships?' This simple function, that can give such exquisite relief, is taken too much for granted. 'I ask you,' the young Doc went on, warming to his theme, 'does a single pump ship of the many you have had stand out in your mind above all others?'

At the time, I had never considered Jimmy Riddling from this angle but now, as I approach my 140,000th, the answer to that question is an emphatic 'Yes'. Two do.

At the tender age of fourteen I was a skinny, undersized, highly strung runt of a boy, a cadet on board HMS *Worcester*. Three years later I found myself indentured on a ship bound from Calcutta to New York loaded with a Far Eastern general cargo, still skinny, still runtish and irredeemably cackhanded.

A careful watch had to be kept on the temperature in the holds as some of this merchandise was prone to spontaneous combustion. It was the job of us apprentices to read and record the temperature from thermometers that hung down the ventilators from the end of lines. This task was performed every few hours.

At about four o'clock on a bitterly cold January afternoon, when the ship was two days steaming from New York, I found the temperature in Number 5 hold had risen to 175 degrees Fahrenheit. I recorded the reading and took the book to the Officer of the Watch. He cast a perfunctory glance down the columns of figures until his gaze was arrested by this abnormally high reading. 'This is bloody impossible ' he said. 'Trust you to make a bollocks of it. Go and read the damn thing again and this time get it right.'

In due course I returned to the bridge and admitted that my first reading must have been wrong as the thermometer now showed some 300 degrees. I then added, 'I don't suppose it's of any significance but I thought you might like to know that smoke is coming out of the ventilator.'

In fact the cargo in the hold was on fire.

We succeeded in making New York without assistance although the seat of the fire became such an inferno that the engineers were unable to use the tunnel to lubricate the propeller shaft bearings. On reaching harbour we were met by a flotilla of firefighting tugs and floats and escorted to a shallow water quay on a remote part of Staten Island.

As soon as the ship was made fast those Yankee firefighters went to town. They removed all the ventilator plugs and shoved hoses into each shaft, and the pumping continued until the entire hull was filled with water to the level of the hatch coamings.

When the ship settled softly on the bottom the fire was well and truly extinguished. The Captain and officers found accommodation ashore whilst the remainder of the crew were signed off and shipped back to England. My fellow apprentices and myself, because of the terms of our indentures, were not easily disposable. We were dumped in the Mission to Seamen until a decision was made about our future.

It was not long before someone came up with the bright idea of employing us as ship's watchmen, thus saving the company the expense of hiring one from on shore. Although the ship was virtually uninhabitable she was still a valuable piece of property that some unfortunate illegitimate had to keep an eye on.

The routine worked out for us necessitated one boy sleeping on board every night in the apprentices cabin. We were provided with an oil stove, to avoid freezing to death in the sub-zero temperatures, and with the usual oil lamp in gimbals to illuminate the encircling gloom. The jetty to which the ship was made fast formed the top of a capital T, with the stalk of the T leading to the shore almost a quarter of a mile away. There was a tramway stop and an all-night café where the quay joined solid ground. The electric tram conveyed us to and from the Mission, and it became the practice of the apprentice coming on for the night to have a good meal in the café before making the long trek down the jetty to spend his lonely night on the half-sunken ship.

The weather was exceptionally severe even for mid-winter in New York, where thirty or more degrees of frost are not unknown. Great plates of thick and dirty ice bumped and crunched against the hull as they moved about the harbour on the ebb and flow of the tide. The grinding of these icy collisions, the solitude, the darkness and the intensity of the cold were unnerving and I came to dread my stint as watchman.

It was a particularly cold and stormy night with the wind blowing from the frozen north when I awoke bursting for 'pump ship'. Befuddled by sleep I clawed from beneath a mountain of blankets clad only in pyjamas. By the light of the oil lamp I rushed from the cabin just in time to release the pent up stream into the scuppers.

Immediately the intensity of the cold struck me like a physical blow, wrapping itself about my scantily clad body and exhausting its heat at an alarming rate. The one thought in my mind was to regain the warmth of the cocoon of blankets from which I had emerged.

A sudden crash told me that the cabin door, which I had flung open in such haste, had blown shut. I was locked out. In the urgency of the moment I had forgotten to sneck up the tongue of the Yale lock and the door stood implacably shut before me. The horror of the situation engulfed me. I knew I must succumb to the cold before I could get even half-way to the all-night café. I panicked. I seized the brass door handle in both hands and tugged at it with every ounce of my strength. The door was solid, built to withstand waves breaking over the ship. My efforts at forcing an entry with bare hands were as futile as farting against thunder.

With enormous effort I regained a degree of self-control. I realised that my chances of survival outside, measured in time, were but a matter of minutes. My only hope of access to the cabin lay in forcibly removing the brass ventilator that covered a six-inch diameter hole at the top of the door. If I could do that then I might push my arm into the hole and grasp the milled knob of the lock and turn it to withdraw the sneck. For security the ventilator was screwed to the door from the inside. I tried pushing at it in the hope that the screws might yield but my efforts were in vain.

In spite of the cold I took off my pyjama jacket and wrapped it round my clenched fist and punched that stubborn piece of brass with all the force I could muster, but to no avail. The physical agony I suffered from the cold is beyond the scope of descriptive writing. I recall the hopeless feeling of life being sucked from me when, suddenly, like St Paul on the road to Damascus, I remembered having seen a small metal tool on the hatch at the foot of the well deck that the Glaswegian carpenter called a spoogel bar'. It was an implement about two feet in length with a pair of claws at one end and a curved chisel at the other. Would it still be there?

Clad in pyjama trousers and slippers I climbed down into the well deck and groped around on the hatch with hands that could feel only pain. They closed round the divinely revealed 'spoogel bar' and the metal froze to my skin as though coated with glue. The ascent of the steel ladder to the bridge deck was like trying to scale the Matterhorn. Even the normally simple act of breathing became an intolerable exertion, but somehow I regained the cabin door.

With every ounce of strength remaining in my body I jabbed at the brass ventilator. Suddenly the screws were torn from the wood and the ventilator disappeared into the cabin followed by the 'spoogel bar' as it flew from my nerveless hands.

Now I could get my arm through the hole in the door and with the tips of my fingers touch the top of the lock. But stretch and strain as I would, I could not reach the milled knob to unlatch the door. Terrifying symptoms of approaching death manifested themselves like patches of light and darkness as consciousness came and went from my brain. A forlorn human heap, I slumped at the foot of what had now become the door to life itself.

As in a trance I saw the end of a rope hitched to a bulwark stay and leading over the side of the ship. Attached to the outboard end would be a cork fender. If I could get that fender inboard it would serve as a step and give the extra height I needed to reach the knob of the lock.

I crawled to the ship's side and pulled myself upright. Then began the painful haul of dragging the fender over the bulwarks. At last it came, a frozen lump that fell to the deck like a cannon ball. I rolled it to the foot of the door then, standing on top of it, pushed my arm through the hole once more.

At last I could reach the unlatching knob. With frost-bitten fingers I turned the sneck and the door swung open. I fell into the cabin and the door crashed to behind me. Driven by the desperate need for self-preservation, I reached my goal, and all feeling was snuffed from me like the blowing out of a candle.

Deep drifts of snow delayed the arrival of my fellow apprentices until after midday. They unlocked the door and came into the cabin where the sound of their voices brought me back to current events. They spotted the brass ventilator cover and the 'spoogel bar' on the cabin floor and asked me what the hell I had been doing.

I said the cabin had become stuffy with the heat from the oil stove and I had found it necessary to remove the ventilator.

One of the lads picked up the battered piece of brass and reminded me sarcastically that there were such things as screwdrivers. The others laughed, and one of them said, 'Trust him to make a bollocks of it.' Only now do I confess to the 'pump ship' that nearly finished me off, the worst one I ever had.

That was in 1926. Thirty-two years later I was invited to a grand shipping dinner. The evening started well. A kind friend had given me a bottle of Burgundy, Chambolle Musigny of an excellent vintage. I decided to drink it while dressing, carefully arraying myself in full evening dress with miniature medals and campaign stars.

The effect of the wine was magical, as I found when I emerged from my hotel into the soft golden sunlight of a London summer evening.

There was ample time before I was due at the banqueting hall and I decided to stroll leisurely down the Strand. My vinous time machine lifted me gently backward to the eighteenth century and I saw myself in the company of James Boswell as he set off to drink his way across London, eyeing the girls as he went.

On arrival at my destination, I divested myself of my light coat and top hat and ascended the noble staircase that branched in two directions from its first landing to facilitate protocol. Concealed lighting illumined the portraits of remote predecessors who stared haughtily from their golden frames. After being announced, and shaking hands with my hosts, I passed into the court room to mingle with my fellow guests and sip pre-dinner glasses of sherry; very dry.

I was dazzled by the row upon row of medals that bedecked the chests of the distinguished company of seafarers and shipping folk and by the galaxy of stars worn nonchalantly upon almost every coat but mine. The blue and red sashes stood in diagonal splendour across the snow-white background of boiled shirts like some splendid dance of drink-befuddled Union Jacks.

Presently word went round that we were to be honoured by the presence of the great man himself. He arrived late, delayed no doubt by the affairs of state, and almost at once the mellifluous voice of the master of ceremonies announced: 'My lords and gentlemen, dinner is served.'

We entered the subdued light of the magnificent dining hall to the strains of 'The Roast Beef of Old England' issuing from the musicians' gallery. There was nothing haphazard about our seating. We all took our places according to a carefully thought out table plan and I discovered myself sandwiched between a rear-admiral and a captain, RN. The great man, of course, occupied the place of honour at the top table.

The meal started with clear turtle soup and the first of the battery of glasses was filled with Dry Sack. Next came half a lobster, to be washed down by Hock Rüdesheimer Riesling 1955 Deinhard. By now we were warming to our gustation and conversation that had begun as a subdued murmur rose to a clamour that vied with the musicians in the gallery.

After an exchange of opinions with the admiral, who had

served as a Flag Officer in Hong Kong, on the relative merits of athwartship oriental ladies and their fore and aft occidental sisters, I turned to find myself confronted with enormous sticks of asparagus with melted butter, which in their turn gave place to Tournedos Maître d'Hôtel with French fried potatoes and courgettes, the whole accompanied by Veuve Clicquot Ponsardin 1949. The penultimate gastronomic delectation came in the guise of Millefeuilles Parisiennes served with bumper glasses of Tuke Holdsworth 1924 port.

The sounds of merriment reached a crescendo and the orchestra, abandoning the unequal struggle, retired gracefully from the gallery. Our gourmandising reached its final stage with a veritable cornucopia of exotic fruits, and the meal took on the quality of a dream as we sipped the Delamain thirty-year-old cognac which was served alongside our coffee.

At length, after the fashion of the miraculous abatement of the storm on the sea of Galilee, the master of ceremonies brought silence with his gavel. There would be a ten-minute interval, he announced, before the loyal toast and the speeches.

I am not aware that my bladder is weaker than the next man's and so I conclude that it was the Burgundy I had imbibed while dressing that urged me to take full opportunity of this timely respite. I rose from my chair and made my way towards the ornate doors which pointed the way towards the cloakroom.

On reaching the point of no return, half way between my seat and the exit, I became aware of an uncanny silence where rightly there should have been a genteel stampede towards the 'heads'. I stopped in my tracks and turned, to find to my horror that a hundred pairs of eyes were fixed stonily upon me. Of all the assembled company, myself apart, only the grand old man was taking this opportunity to make himself comfortable.

How was I to know that the break in proceedings had been inserted for his special benefit? Everyone else seemed to know, and there was I, desperate and alone, standing like an idiot in Limbo. Every instinct told me to bolt back to my place and pretend that I had misunderstood, but with great force of character I subdued this mad idea and proceeded, without haste and with all the dignity I could muster, towards the swing doors.

I waited to hold them open for the most famous war hero since Nelson. He approached with painful slowness, aided by his stick. I was engulfed by my selfconsciousness, aware that beads of sweat glistened on my face and coursed in rivulets down my body beneath my hard-boiled shirt. At the appropriate moment I pulled the doors open and he passed down the corridor ahead of me.

As close as I dared, I took station on his port quarter and

adjusted my speed to his shuffling gait until we reached the lavatory door. Again I took on the rôle of doorman to allow the great man to pass ahead of me. He emitted the growl of an old bulldog, which I took to mean 'Thank you'. Then, side by side, we took our places before the vitreous basins and our ballast splashed down to meet and mingle in the trough at our feet and disappear down a common scupper. I searched my mind desperately for some bright remark, but concluded that, in the circumstances, conversation was not essential.

As we washed our hands he spoke. The voice was old but it was still the voice that lashed our flagging spirits in the 1940s and inspired the effort that secured victory in that great human conflict. He said: 'My boy, let me give you some advice. Always have a pump ship when the opportunity presents itself because you can never be sure of the next one.'

I thanked him. Together we made our way back to the banqueting hall, now in line abreast. I walked to my place and took my seat at the table, and the admiral, leaning over towards me, said, 'Captain, if you ever write your memoirs don't forget to include the great WC encounter.' I include it now — the best pump ship I ever had.

Woman at Sea
Lily Brown-Try

I began my life at sea in 1959 at the age of 38. British companies turned me down as a stewardess. So did the college at South Shields when I said I wanted to train as a radio officer — even though I pointed out that Victoria Drummond had sailed as a chief engineer during the war. Eventually the Norwegians took me.

Ignorance is bliss. I proved to be the only woman on board; the chief steward did not sober up for a week; and I had never served a meal before. Every morning I had to take coffee to the Captain but one morning — six months after I had joined — he had a new idea, perhaps because the coffee was not very good. I thought then that it was time to leave.

Back in England my first thought was 'No more for me; never again!' But after three months I grew restless. This time I was away for two years. There were two other women on this ship and we worked for a good chief steward, so occasionally we had a half-day ashore. I visited many Flying Angel clubs all over the world and received and exchanged books: it was heaven after a day's work to be able to lose oneself in a book. I joined in the teaching of English on board and the classes were well attended. I even learned to dance at sea. And then there was the sewing and the ironing! Slop chest garments never seemed to fit well and after slop chest nights I always knew I would get first one and then another member of the crew cornering me and saying, 'Could you just fix this?' If you did it for one, you had to do it for the lot. A ship is worse than any village for gossip, so no special favours were possible.

There was no air-conditioning in the tropics in those days. It was hard on the feet being a stewardess and sheer bliss to go under the shower at the end of the day's work and then lie flat on the deck of the cabin with one's feet propped up on a pulled-out drawer. Then there were the times when a passage was prolonged and the water ran short: sheer joy then to have a tropical rainstorm and to run on deck and feel the rain on one's face while everything available was put to catch the water.

Crossing the line could be fun — even if you did have to drink those vile concoctions, be daubed with grease, and flung in a hatch filled with water.

When the names of different countries appear in the news now I hark back to my own memories of them — the 'rodeo' in Uruguay, the drive through Brazil . . . I was terrified when, after bargaining with the taxi-driver in Vittoria, he drove off the main road and through a shanty town. There was no way of getting out of the taxi. The driver had a handle which he produced and inserted from the outside when he wanted to open the door. I tried to muster all my Spanish and explain that I wasn't a tourist but a merchant sailor, displaying my calloused hands. When at last he understood, the driver broke into a toothy grin — it was like the sun coming out — and began to tell me about his wife and house and the children.

Japan offered an altogether different way of life. It was difficult to realise you were actually seeing Mount Fuji and that it wasn't a coloured postcard. The politely giggling girls wanted to touch my blond hair to make sure it was real. The schoolboys wanted to try out their English. There was old Japan, and modern Japan, with fantastic service in the shops, and the international Expo pavilions. 'Auld Lang Syne' Japanese-style is something I shall never forget.

I was lucky enough to be in Canada for their international exhibition too — there was so much to see that I never sat down. Then there was a New Year's Day in Fremantle, the sands so hot that you could not walk barefoot, and the surfers coming in on the immense breakers: the breeze blowing to Perth was called the 'Fremantle doctor'. Sydney and Newcastle also have their marvellous beaches, while Port Hedland was just like a Western movie set — wide rough streets with dancing outside and a fight in between and then all friends again.

One time I saw Stromboli spewing fire into an inky sky. We climbed Vesuvius and peered into the grey crater to see steam hissing from the crevices. I wish I could go to Pompeii again, and Odessa — even if they did introduce anti-American propaganda into the ballet. The humble ball-point pen and, of course, cigarettes were sought after on my first visit, but gradually there was more and more in the shops, and more attractive fashions. Visiting a Russian ship in India we were shown American films and given caviar on fresh baked bread.

Of course there were other times: fire in the engine-room, and I could not swim; the second mate found half in and half out of his cabin on the deck, dead and only thirty-two; the pumpman who was gassed, and my trying to help. When I saw the piece of wood slipping from between the pumpman's teeth I put my fingers there. He bit so hard that I knew there was hope for him.

When we had the explosion on the supertanker all I could contribute was prayer. It was during a storm and because of the weather we could only have launched one of the two lifeboats. I gathered all the women — two wives as well as the three crew — and we brewed tea while the men donned asbestos suits. For six hours we were in the cabin with lifebelts on. Even when the fire was put out in the control room we were still not sure there would be no further explosion. In that area two other Norwegian ships had gone down inside an hour. One vanished without trace; from the other one a single survivor was found on a raft three days afterwards — he was the most powerful swimmer on board. We had sailed twice with the bosun of the ship that vanished without trace.

A glamorous and exciting life? Well, not exactly. You slept on the deck rather than be thrown out of your bunk in a storm. You listened to the creaking and groaning of the ship and to the whistling and howling of the wind and the boom–boom–boom of heavy seas against the ship's sides and you thought, 'Heaven help the sailor on a night like this.' But, oh the glory of the calm after the storm, and the setting sun, and a bright night of stars dancing above a shimmering sea! And then, too, there were times when you felt useful — looking after a captain with con-cussion and a broken leg; sitting with someone who had gone crazy; even painting on deck, or just doing your job.

In 1975 the doctor said I had high blood pressure and could only work on ferries; but ferries were not light work. One day I was so tired that, climbing up to a top bunk, I fell and hit the corner of a table and broke three ribs. For a few days I tried to carry on, hardly daring to breathe, but finally I had to report to the doctor. I had broken a wrist and broken a shoulder before, but the broken ribs were the worst.

And that was that. 'No more seafaring', they decreed, and now I am just a 'land crab' — as we used to call the passengers on the ferry — gazing out over Oslo fjord and thinking of the past. I wouldn't have missed it for anything.

Fog
Bill Meneight

Where I live I can hear plainly the sounds from Liverpool Bay and the river. In the fall of the year, when the skies are so often grey with melancholy and the street lamps are wreathed in mist, the mournful wails of the fog signals from ship and shore come floating over the desolate sand dunes and, softly but insistently, they call me away.

In an instant of time I am out there, questing and peering; for fog is blindness, or perhaps it is a thousand wisps of clinging mist which bind the giant with Lilliputian cunning and make him helpless. One can admire, even though one may fear, a storm at sea. The very intensity of it, the howling demoniacal shrieks of the wind, the driven spume, the insensate fury of the seas as they pile up and crash down can conjure up admiration and awe, even while the belly screws up into its smallest compass in fear. But there is nothing to admire in a fog. It snares its victims, not like a storm boldly and forthright, but coldly and under the grey cloak of invisibility. It is insidious and, while it lasts, it is forever.

I say it is forever, for after a few hours of it one can conceive of no other world. It saps the mind and robs it of comparison, save only that by night the great arch of light spreads out and down from the foremast meeting the upward sweep of the sidelights until the watcher is enclosed inside a white glare, at which he gazes unseeingly.

I have endured fog for four days and nights. Long before the end I was in a world completely divorced from any known world, It was inchoate, grey and void of reality, a swirling mass, time-less and amorphous. Hour after hour, the ship, unnatural in its misty shroud, pushed softly through the dimly seen water. Only the plash of the bow wave and the raucous blare of the siren broke the fog-bound silence. Few words were spoken, the officer-of-the-watch usually stood frozen into immobility, save for the occasional tug at the whistle lanyard, and the lookout, crouched in the bows, gazed ahead into nothingness thinking, I suppose, all sorts of private thoughts, and waiting for his relief. My legs carried me seven paces up, seven paces down; up and down, up and down. It was better to walk than stand although in the end my legs ached intolerably.

In a fog thoughts are jumbled up. One is intensely aware of a drop of water constantly forming and dripping from a rope's end, and the intervals between the blasts on the whistle are an eternity. The mind wryly recalls the rude awakening, the telegraph jangling its 'stand-by' signal to the engine-room and the reluctant voice of the officer of the watch saying 'It's come in thick, sir', followed immediately by a blast on the siren. That is as it should be, but long before the regulation two minutes' interval has elapsed the whistle is blown again, and by the time some clothes have been scrambled on, it has blown again. It is a very human reaction, for the officer is up there on the bridge and, until the Master arrives, he is responsible for the safety of the ship and crew, so he blows the whistle long and often. Now, it is different: the fog has been around quite some time, and in any case the Old Man has her and the intervals between the blasts become longer. Finally I have to say, 'Keep her blowing, Mister,' and the interval returns to normal.

The hours merge; there are more people on the bridge; a huddle of figures and low voices betoken the end of a watch. There is a cup of tea and a parting 'Good night, sir', from the retiring mate. In deference to my vigil, he tries to inject some sympathy into his voice but his relief is obvious. The new officer of the watch is reluctant but resigned, and alert after sleep. The whistle blows with even regularity for the first hour or so — and then gradually, the intervals lengthen. 'Keep her blowing, Mister.'

A curtain of swirling fog, illumined by mast head and side lights, imposes an intolerable strain on the eyes. There is no relief save that at times, and momentarily only, the lights are switched off in an endeavour to gauge the visibility — if any. A rich dark blackness bathes the eyes, and the whole body relaxes. It would be so much more restful to leave it so; but even though they shine but a few yards around the ship, the lights must go on.

It is at night that the imagination takes over. Visions of a forecastle full of men asleep, and always a ship bearing down on them, unseen and unheard. How to get them out in time — given time? The shambles if one did not. Silly, impossible solutions pass through the mind and then one becomes conscious of a deep fatigue. The ache from the legs passes upwards through the spine and meets the ache at the shoulders. They have been such constant companions that one has grown accustomed to their presence. To be able to sleep, to straighten out the bones and sinews so inextricably mingled, would be worth forfeiting that doubtful seat in heaven.

As the night passes, the glare lessens and a dull opaqueness is substituted; the ship comes to life, muted life. The bosun arrives on the bridge and the mate turns with relief from peering into the formless face of the fog. They mutter together, and presumably the day's work is fixed. In retrospect, I see in my mind's eye the ghoulish vision I had conjured up in the graveyard hours, the gory, mangled bodies, the twisted steel, and the fleeing figures limned in the ghostly glow. I can smile now at the thought, for daylight, even miserable grey light, brings sanity and some perspective.

One of the most beautiful sights in the world is, in my eyes, the rolling away of a fog bank, revealing an undisturbed view of a sun-dappled sea to the limits of a far horizon. Once, and only once, do I remember being captured by the beauty of fog itself. It was after twenty-four hours of tense watch, for we were in the traffic lanes. The sun had risen and it hung above the low-lying fog in a sky more blue by comparison. We waited, listened, and watched hopefully until, suddenly, by some freak of air currents, the ship was in the centre of a mile-wide, blue and sparkling sea. Out on the circumference several avenues of blue water, bounded by towering cliffs of fog, escaped to the horizon. The fog cliffs, of pearly sheen and shot with iridescent colour, were sheer and firm in outline. There was no merging with the deep blue of the water or the immaculate sky. The avenues seemed to lead to enchantment.

Leave

Chris Lee

It starts with me sitting in the back seat of a taxi with my luggage tucked away in the boot.

As the taxi drives away, I turn to view my ship through the rear window. As the distance between the ship and the taxi increases, so the ship appears to get smaller. It looks good.

Tired and happy, I arrive home to be greeted by my wife and young children, and in the next few hours I try to pick up the threads of the shore life which I dropped at the end of my last leave. That evening I bath the children, put them to sleep, do the washing up after supper, and so to bed.

Not too much to bed though for throughout the night the children wake up in turn and I find myself putting them back to bed, having provided comfort both spiritual and material. My fragmented night ends around six o'clock as the children decide it is time to be up and about. While I feel as if I have had less sleep than I might have had watchkeeping, my wife has somehow managed to sleep the night through in the security of my home-coming and rouses herself reluctantly just enough to sit up in bed and drink the cup of tea I bring her at seven-thirty.

By the time she is up and dressed, I have cooked the breakfast and, after it is devoured, I just have time to do the washing up before dressing the children. At this time my wife is usually talking to her mother on the telephone: mother-in-law's sense of timing is impeccable.

The house tidied up, I turn my attention to the garden — two acres of primeval forest and swamp. Nature has made a mockery of my efforts of last leave, and with machete, scythe and flame gun I attack thistles, willowherb, bramble, goosegrass and nightshade with more enthusiasm than skill. Occasionally I recognise something I actually planted the previous year, albeit somewhat stunted and a host to blackfly and other garden pests. By the time I fully realise just how flabby and out of condition I have become during the last voyage it is lunchtime. For the third time that morning I rescue my son from the goldfish pond — and note its declining population. Then I save the cats from further torment by removing my daughter.

Muddy boots off and hands washed, I eat lunch and, after washing up, dress the children in a second lot of clean clothes. It is time to replenish the depleted larder.

Shopping in a large and crowded supermarket with two active youngsters can be full of fun and surprises. My son removes the bottom can in a pyramidal display and I try to smile amiably as the assistants rush to clear up the mess. Leaving the trolley for a moment, I turn to see my daughter, who is sitting in it, propelling herself along the racks by pulling on the shelves, scattering catfood and tins of soup as she goes.

Home again, I make the tea. Soon it will be bathtime and bedtime again and I can look forward to a long and relaxing evening — knocking up a few shelves in the cellar and fitting double-glazing to reduce the heat bills.

During my leave I will entertain, and be entertained by, numerous friends and relatives, few of whom my wife sees while I am at sea. Being of a declining and emigrating race, I have few relatives myself. My wife makes up for this. Most of my friends are of an ex-nautical nature; my wife's date from teaching days. When we meet again, there is much catching up to do and sometimes I find it amazing that life, with its manifold complications, goes on all the time that I am shut away in my small world at sea.

When we can afford the petrol we sometimes go out to see the countryside or shops further afield. Since my wife does not drive, this is something that can only be done when I am at home. It is amazing how much more interesting she seems to find the shops in other towns.

And so the days go by. Eventually the garden is more like a meadow than a jungle. I nearly finish painting the house. The towel rails in the bathroom have been fixed back to the wall for the tenth time. Then, all too soon, it is time to return to my ship. Once again I am sitting in my taxi, my luggage in the boot.

This time I view my ship through the front window. As the distance between the ship and the taxi decreases, so the ship appears to get larger. It looks good.

And the Girl he leaves behind him

Jenny Penson

Most seafarers are probably unaware that they are married to the ideal wife. Having swopped experiences with other wives in the same boat (to coin a phrase), I would like to draw the attention of seafaring husbands to the things that go on when they are away from home.

The ideal seafarer's wife is as faithful as a bloodhound, as independent as a long-distance runner, as practical as Barry Bucknell, and as well-adjusted as Lassie. She has to be. The difficulties she encounters during her husband's absences would send a lesser woman to a solicitor or a psychiatrist, or maybe to both.

First she has to convince herself that a conventional life is not necessarily the happiest one. To do this she has to cast off the deeply embedded idea that she should conform to what society thinks is 'normal' or usual — which means having a husband who, if not a completely nine-to-five man, is at least home for weekends, birthdays and Christmas and does not leave the happy matrimonial household for months at a time.

She is up against public opinion when she bravely looks on marriage to a seafarer as an advantage and not as a handicap. She endures that infuriating pity of her well-meaning friends with their nice, safe, weekday-working husbands. 'I just don't know how you cope!', 'It isn't much of a life for you, is it?' From not-so-great friends there comes the subtle implication that anyone who calls that set-up a marriage must have been pretty hard up for a husband! Also lurking somewhere in the conversation is usually a question such as 'Don't you worry when he's so far away?', a question which every wife knows translates to 'Don't sailors still have a girl in every port?'

She soon learns that attack makes her feel much better than being on the defensive all the time. So, remembering the cheering point that there are other husbands who travel away from home sometimes (pilots, executives and salesmen, to name a few), she can indicate that no man needs to go to the extreme of sailing round the world in order to 'sample' other women. A routine office job probably gives a man more scope.

She can then become almost poetic over the joys of those grand reunions, the excited planning and preparations, then the thrill as the ETA (which for those who do not know means 'expected time of arrival') draws near. The prospect of a second honeymoon every few months causes a streak of envy in any routine housewife's heart, and a little envy directed at a seafarer's wife for a change is very good for her morale. And, while more conventional couples are slaving over hot stoves, desks or whatever in order to earn their three weeks' break a year, the seafarer's wife can look forward to umpteen visits and outings in the week as soon as her husband is home.

Having learned that most social events are a depressing example of the Noah's Ark principle — that is, guests are only invited in matching pairs, male and female of each kind — the ideal wife has to turn to other pursuits to counter her loneliness. She usually becomes frantically busy, throwing herself with generous abandon into the community around her, becoming the number one dispenser of tea and sympathy, a kind of universal aunt. With such energy and enthusiasm, not to mention spare time, she is the perfect target when it comes to voting people on to committees.

The seafarer's wife also copes admirably with all the chores which are commonly regarded as male prerogatives. She can change plugs, paper the ceiling and stoke up the boiler, and take in her stride all those nasty crises which occur the moment her husband has departed for a 'little' six-month trip. As all seafarers' wives know, it is at that moment that the roof begins to leak, the sink blocks up and the car refuses to start.

When writing letters to her husband, she is often torn between not wishing to alarm him (knowing what ancient history it will be by the time he reads it) and a strong need to unburden the trivialities of daily living on to someone else. The sort of day when the baby develops colic, the toddler discovers the coal bucket, the dog is sick on the new carpet and the washing machine overflows all over the kitchen, does offer extreme provocation. But being an ideal wife, she does not seek solace with the window-cleaner or the whisky bottle, and she manages to write a cheerful account of the day as if it had all been great fun.

The seafarer who reads this will be amazed to learn that he is married to such a paragon, for all these qualities have to come to the fore when he is away. He is probably quite unaware that such a versatile genius is hiding behind the helpless female he comes home to. Even an ideal wife needs a rest from such efficiency, and part of the joy of having her husband home is to be able to surrender all these responsibilities to him for a while, in particular the unenviable task of being the omnipotent parent. For if the patter of tiny feet is heard in the home, remember that the seafarer's wife has to cope with the exhausting job of trying to be both parents at once. If those feet happen to be large ones, it is even more difficult, for she may be faced with all kinds of complex personal questions plus problems of discipline which she will be only too glad to refer to her husband whenever she is lucky enough to see him.

It may appear from what has been said that a career-minded ideal wife has a less complicated time. But she too has conflicts to resolve. For instance, if she is climbing the ladder of success in her job, should she throw away her good prospects by ensuring she is free whenever the sailor is home from the sea?

Having elaborated on all these difficulties which are just a part of being a seafarer's wife, the reader may be surprised to learn that there is some compensation. The compensation, is, of course, the husband: for it is generally agreed among us seafarers' wives that if only they were at home more often seafarers would make ideal husbands.

The Dreaded Bay
Wilson Money

We had enjoyed the bull-fighting programme on Sunday afternoon television off Acapulco and we were approaching the Bay
of Tehuantepec at our prescribed speed when the forecast gave
the news. The Bay was acting up again.

By the time I turned in after an early watch the ship was
beginning to pitch and roll. The spray was slapping against my
window of splinterproof glass which faced forward, and the
window over my bunk on the starboard side was also getting its
share of salt water. You may have read of ships tossing like corks.
We were soon tossing like a cork.

It was not long before the doors began to swing and bang and
everyone not on watch was doing as I was — bouncing on foam
rubber and praying 'Please don't let my window smash.' Steel
shutters were supplied, but always by the time the operation
became necessary it was too late to carry it out.

Approximately ten thousand tons of ship plus cargo was
bobbing up and down like a yo-yo, except that a yo-yo keeps a
smooth and regular motion. Our motion was neither smooth nor
regular. It was jerky and violent, irregular and turbulent and my
dentures in their tumbler were chattering and complaining like a
skeleton with the palsy. After one particularly spine-fracturing
jolt there was an almighty crash in the alleyway outside my room
and after a moment's thought I realised what it was. On both the
port and starboard corridors there were recesses in which fire
extinguishers were slung. One of them had jumped from its
hook and was rolling about on the deck outside our cabins like a
primed bomb.

It is a quirk of human nature that when something like that
happens, in the circumstances of that time, no-one wants to
know. I lay on my bed of nails; the second mate lay on his; and
the first mate lay on his. Each one of us was waiting for the other
to leap to his feet and spur himself into action. The Old Man had,

no doubt, already left his superior but more dangerous double bed. He would be on the bridge, wedged in a corner of the wheelhouse opposite the third mate, both of them straining to remain on their feet as the ship lurched and staggered.

Beneath our deck lay numerous engineer officers, also swearing and cursing, and asking themselves why some lazy idiot among the navigators did not get up and do something about that half-hundredweight of fire extinguisher which was careering to and fro like a wartime doodlebug when the engine had cut out. Had we been drinking and singing with a bunch of dancing girls they would have been up on our deck like a shot, complaining that they could not sleep. Now, when they certainly could not sleep, they were all playing 'possum. Inevitably, on an exceptionally vicious roll, the madcap extinguisher slid athwartships, like a crazily computerised torpedo, and slammed head on into the Old Man's door, thereby activating the plunger in its nose.

That did it! Not only did the steel drum race up and down the U-shaped alleyway, knocking paint and cobs of timber from bulkheads, but the foaming fluid from its interior squirted furiously from its hose, whipping round and spitting CO_2 like venom from an enraged cobra. When, at one bell, the standby man arrived to call the second mate, he met it head on, and was immediately smothered like a cream puff, losing his footing in the slime, and joining the cause of the disaster in sliding, skipping and skating to and fro across the accommodation. Only then did the occupants of the adjacent cabins emerge and assist in the fantastic custard pie-flinging pantomime in the course of which four fast and furious fellows succeeded at last in capturing the runaway and lashing it back to its home base, mopping up the mess in some measure while the exhausted extinguisher still spurted faintly like some languishing Lothario.

With great difficulty the second mate peeled off his wringing pyjamas, dressed for duty and clambered aloft. The mate and I wiped off the scum from our bodies with wet flannels — more could not be done in the conditions prevailing — and, rolling on our bunks, we wriggled into fresh night clothing, to lie cursing and praying for some respite.

Ever since joining that ship I had intended to soft-soap Chippy into building me a rack in my wardrobe to secure my rum and cordial bottles and cans of beer, but of course I had never got around to it, so that night found me — as usual in such circumstances — with two bottles of liquor jammed between the corners of the mattress and the woodwork at my head and a bottle of cordial and another of carbonated lemonade in similar positions at my feet. I was determined to keep them there come hell or high water.

But the Bay defeated me. During one more gigantic convulsion as, with a shattering bone-jarring crash, the bows smashed the next wave into a row of rollers, the lemonade bottle flew from its nest into the air and smashed on the cabin deck with a splintering explosion. Another crisis! Shattered glass everywhere. Slippers slithering up and down out of reach with every billow. Glass in my bunk. Glass in my hair. Glass in my feet. How was I to manoeuvre myself out of my bunk, cautiously and in slow motion, while being bucked up and down like a ping pong ball on a shooting fountain?

Then came a horrible frightening thought. Was everything safe, sound and secure in the wireless room?

Grabbing my slippers as they slithered past, I tried to shake out the slivers of glass that had lodged inside and gingerly inserted my toes. Have you ever observed how tiny splinters of glass stick everywhere? There was a little pain, a little blood — did I have any plasters in my washbasin cabinet, I wondered; but first aid would have to wait. Tossing my legs over the leeboard at the wrong moment, I was thrown like a sack of potatoes against the bulkhead. I grasped the washbasin for support, braced my legs far apart, and hung on. Then, bouncing from wall to wall, I staggered along the alleyway and, step by step, climbed on hands and knees to the wireless room, unlatched the door, and stumbled inside with no bones broken.

The typewriter — a heavy, office job — I had stupidly left on a table by the after bulkhead. Despite its rubber pads, it had already fractured the fiddle on the port side and was teetering towards the edge. I put both hands and my weight on it and awaited my chance. I knew my ship. I had once stood right there, holding a cup of tea, and I had placed the tea on that same table while reaching for a book on the shelf which was level with my head. And before I could drop my hands again the ship had leapt into the air, swiped the cup out of reach, and hurled it to the floor, where it failed to bounce. This time I lifted and dropped my burden on the deck at the propitious moment, and I lashed it to the table legs — which were bolted to the deck — with a length of insulated wire. Then I spread out my arms and legs and looked about me. All was well so far: spares were safe in their holes and racks; my own portable typewriter was locked in a drawer; nothing seemed loose anywhere.

Sitting on my bruised rear and moving gingerly from step to step, I worked my way below again. Solid salt water still battered my window at each thundering dive and, after the dive, we would swoop into the heavens by express service until the ship was almost perpendicular and I was standing on my head. My remaining bottles had now been stuffed under the mattress, and my right hand was gripping the hook that normally held my travelling clock — the clock itself, well wrapped in a shirt, was in one of the drawers. My left hand clutched the washstand, which was firmly riveted to the bulkhead.

And so it went on and on. A thousand tons of ocean would hit the forefoot. Then would come the sickening sweep, a ride on a super figure-of-eight railway with a neckbreaking swerve at the peak, though you never knew which way, followed by another bonebreaking descent to twenty thousand leagues under the sea as my lacerated feet slapped the bottom bunkboard and I stood on my heels while the ship's stem sliced into the next roller, half of which swept along the foredeck and thundered against the midship housing, shaking the vessel to her very keelson and all but flinging me head first into the window. I stared at the glass in fascination, praying that it would withstand the massive impact, and that the bolts of my washstand would take the strain of my 160 pounds of fearful flesh and blood.

The tortured timbers and girders groaned and creaked, and thuds, clashes, bangs, screams and curses came from all sides. And then, right above my head, came the crunch to end all crunches. 'Oh, God,' I thought, 'my main transmitter's gone for a Burton.'

Once more I retrieved my slippers, this time raking out the glass with the handle of a toothbrush before inserting my feet. Jet-propelled from wall to wall like a rag doll, and thrown up the companionway, I scrabbled back to the radio room. It was not the transmitter. The office typewriter had taken charge. Its weight had torn the table away from its bolts and impelled it like a tank into and through the beaverboard which lined the cabin. At that point, fortunately, it had jammed.

I gave in. The office chair was securely bolted to a beam, so there I wedged my weary body and, legs braced well apart, rested my head on my arms on the wedged desk. Thus anchored, I awaited the dawn, ready at any moment to pump out an SOS. The Bay of Tehuantepec, I decided, would be crossed off my visiting list.

North Atlantic Car-carrier
Brian McManus

Arctic Troll lay berthed alongside a Thames-side wharf next to Ford's at Dagenham when I joined her with my wife Hazel in December. Even in the winter twilight her 200 yards of orange hull made an impressive impact on this dingy part of London. *Arctic Troll* is 602 feet long and 87 feet wide. Her Swiss-built Sulzer engine — Sulzer is the Rolls-Royce of marine diesels — drives her through the water at 16½ knots. To achieve this it develops 20,000 horse power and to cover her 396 miles in 24 hours she uses 41 tons of fuel. These, however, are nautical miles. Converted into motoring terms it becomes 456 miles in a day and to go one mile she uses 20 gallons of fuel. But then some 35,000 tons of ship and cargo are being pushed along.

Smaller diesels, called auxiliaries, drive the generators which make the ship's electricity for light, radio, radar, gyro compass, fire detectors, steering motors, cooking, washing machines, fridges and pumps. The ship's water is pumped up to the living quarters from storage tanks in the bottom of the ship. Every time a tap is turned on the pump operates. These auxiliaries use 2·75 tons or 616 gallons of fuel a day. In addition, the big Sulzer diesel and auxiliaries together use 10 gallons of lubricating oil. As the ship travels along the waste heat from the engine — which operates at over 400°C — is harnessed to produce steam for heating the crew's quarters, making hot water and distilling the sea-water into drinking water. This shipboard-produced water is the delight of any wives who travel on a voyage as it needs so little washing powder in the washing machines. But it has one fault. Being extremely pure distilled water it may be excellent for a car battery but it does not make a good cup of tea. This is one reason why the popular drink aboard nowadays is instant coffee.

The living quarters are of a high standard and superior to many except the best hotels. Apart from the juniors most officers have their own dayroom with a fridge, bedroom and bathroom.

The junior officers and petty officers share a bathroom between two. There are also officers' and crew bars where draught lager is served at 10p a pint and a large selection of spirits is available. Sweets, chocolates, nuts and crisps can be bought from the catering officer. Cigarettes sell at 10p a packet of 20 and whisky is 80p a bottle! In the bars are international television sets so that no matter where in the world the ship may be she can tune in to local television. Food, like the accommodation, compares well with that of a good hotel, so it is little wonder that the bill to feed the 33 crew for one month is nearly £2,000.

Four Troll ships operate under the Red Ensign and one under the Norwegian flag. They are sophisticated ships each capable of carrying 2,100 cars in seven decks. Once the cars are discharged the decks are pulled back and the holds become suitable for timber, containers, or such bulk cargoes as grain or iron ore. To handle the cargo there are three twin Hagglund cranes. Made in Sweden, the Hagglunds, like the Sulzer, are the Rolls-Royce of ships' cranes and each one costs £175,000. If worked singly the six cranes lift 15 tons each and if worked in tandem each pair lifts 30 tons.

The four British Trolls belong to separate one-ship companies and carry the funnel colours of Wilhelmsen's of Oslo. *Arctic Troll*, however, is the exception and her funnel is adorned with a red-painted troll. She and her three sisters were built at 3 Maj Shipyard, Rijeka, Yugoslavia (3rd May 1945 was Yugoslavia's Liberation Day), for £4 millions each. This was cheap and the cost of building such a ship in 1975 was £21 millions (£40 millions in 1982!). By ordering four ships of the same type from one yard the price might be cut by 15 per cent.

Arctic Troll is owned by the single-ship company, Canpark Shipping Co Ltd, London, a subsidiary of Leitch Transport, Toronto. If you wish to own a ship many governments and shipyards make what shipping men call 'cheap cash' readily available. The formula of such shipowners as the late Aristotle Onassis or the Hong Kong Chinaman C. Y. Pao is simple enough: use subsidized cash from governments or shipyards; find a long-term profitable charter with a reputable firm — Shell or P&O for instance — which is unlikely to go bust; then sit back in some tax haven and count the money coming in.

Arctic Troll was built on this principle. In 1971 an investment grant of 20 per cent was available from the British Government; 10 per cent was put down with the contract which was borrowed against the 20 per cent investment grant; then an 80 per cent mortgage was obtained from a major international bank. Marine Midland, William Brandt, Hambros, Hill Samuel and Kleinwort Benson are some of those specializing in marine finance. Before delivery, if you are really smart, nominal control of the company and the resulting tax allowances can be sold to a British investor for a cash sum of perhaps 20 per cent of the ship's cost. It sounds easy but, although many try, few succeed.

Arctic Troll stayed one night at Dagenham and then sailed for Bremen at 1600 the next afternoon. The 24-hour stay at Dagenham was hectic. With Christmas coming 14 men left and 14 new men joined. It seems always to happen that just as the ship is sailing stores arrive, and this day was no exception. The tide was falling and we needed to leave quickly. Nevertheless the stores, including the Christmas spirits, were put aboard in time.

I never feel I have taken command of a ship until she puts to sea. As the two tugs pulled *Arctic Troll* her engine was moved ahead and astern to coax her round, the engine being controlled from the bridge. As a precaution in confined waters, however, the engineers stand by in the control-room in case the automation fails. Bremen is only 24 hours away and for the 67 miles of the voyage down the Thames and the last 65 miles up the Weser it is compulsory to take a pilot. The weather was good so our supernumerary wives expected a quick fair-weather dash across the North Sea. But the North Sea is not to be trusted and the following morning we were in the teeth of a north-west gale and we were steering north-east. It could not have been worse. The 4,000 tons of cargo remaining aboard was in the bottom of the ship which gave a pendulum effect making the ship roll 35 degrees to port and starboard or a total of 70 degrees. In these conditions it was impossible to cook a meal and lunch that day was sandwiches, but none of our guests complained for, alas, they were all prostrate, stricken with seasickness.

By the time we arrived at the Weser pilot station the gale had not abated and the pilot boat was working in smoother water 20 miles inside the river. However, with typical Teutonic thoroughness a pilot in a shore-based radar station 'talked' us by VHF into the river. The VHF is a radio telephone with a 30-mile range. Luckily for us, English is the language used internationally at sea and many pilots on the Continent are fluent.

From the huge container terminal at Bremerhaven, where the pilot is changed, it is another 32 miles to Bremen. The *Arctic Troll* being more than 20,000 gross tons has to employ two pilots. The land is flat and fertile, the river narrow. As she pushed the ebb tide and needed to slow down when passing dredgers, riverside wharves and shipyards, this last portion of the voyage took four hours.

By the time we were secure at the quay in Bremen it was 0100 on Sunday morning. Time is money in shipping. At 0500 dockers boarded and by noon the 4,000 tons of paper products were discharged.

When the cargo is completely discharged a voyage has ended. Now the repair gangs moved in. They were allotted 24 hours in which to complete their work because at 1500 on Monday afternoon the ship was to sail for Emden to load Volkswagens at 0600 Tuesday morning. In the meantime another ship wanted to berth, so *Arctic Troll* was shifted to a lay-by berth. It was an expensive operation, with two pilots and three tugs, each tug charging £300. The use of the lay-by berth cost £1,600 a day and the repair bill came to £20,000.

Arctic Troll sailed on schedule and arrived at Emden at 0400. Here the new voyage began, and throughout her life the ship has carried Volkswagens from Emden to the east coast of the United States and Canada.

It took three shifts to load the 2,100 vehicles with the Hagglund cranes. Two shifts were worked Tuesday. At 0600 on Wednesday morning the Chief Engineer's wife and two daughters and the Chief Officer's wife left us. In the meantime, the Second Engineer's wife and their six-year-old daughter had embarked. At 1230 on Wednesday loading was completed, and at 1400, with the ship secured for the atrocious weather of the North Atlantic winter, we sailed for Halifax and Baltimore. As we vacated the berth, a car-carrier from Japan was waiting to take our place. She would return to Japan loaded with Volkswagens intended for the west coast of the United States and for Hawaii.

There is a choice of two routes from Emden to Halifax in Canada. Round the north of Scotland through the Pentland Firth is picturesque and shorter than the route I select through the English Channel, but being 500 miles further north the weather will be considerably worse. Even going through the Channel it is impossible to avoid the depressions which form over the frozen Great Lakes every couple of days. These depressions then come rushing eastwards, sometimes at speeds of 60 knots (69mph), causing Force 10 winds (that is 56 to 62mph) as far away as 500 miles from their centres. The North Atlantic is a bad place in winter.

Once out of the Channel there is again a choice of two routes. The great circle route follows the earth's curvature and is the shorter, but it has the disadvantage of sending us further north than our departure point off the Channel Islands to be buffeted by those gales. The better route is the direct straight line, called the Rhumb Line, which adds about 30 miles to the distance. From Emden to Halifax is 3,000 miles on this track or 3,455 motoring miles.

We passed Dover at 0745 on Thursday, the temperature being

2½°C. On Friday we were in a northerly Force 8 (39 to 46 mph) gale and the heavy rolling made our passengers seasick. Otherwise we were quite pleased with the situation because the gale was slightly behind us and not delaying our progress. Our facsimile machine giving us weather reports works in much the same way as that producing a newspaper radio picture, except that its print-outs are of the weather synopsis. The print-out showed that we were on the southern edge of a high pressure system so we knew that as we went further west the gale would veer to the south. The gale continued unabated until Monday but it was always a little astern and we made an average speed of 16·6 knots which for the time of the year and a westbound passage was a record.

Tuesday, 16th December, was the warmest day of the voyage so far, with the temperature reaching 15°C. During the morning it was necessary to stop for three hours and repair a broken fuel pipe.

On Wednesday evening we passed Sable Island, a miserable place. Throughout December the temperature hovers around freezing point. For 12 days of the month on average the island is in the teeth of a gale, and half the winds recorded blow from the polar quadrant, north-west to north-east. During a severe winter the island is surrounded by ice from February until May. Landing is prohibited by the Canadians except in case of necessity — like shipwreck. Sable Island knows plenty about that and is called the 'graveyard of the Atlantic'. Its shores are strewn with the remains of ships which have been fooled by the erratic currents and inadvertently beached themselves during fog to become total losses.

We approached Halifax at 1000 on the 18th December, nearly eight days after leaving Emden. The weather was blowing a southerly gale with sleet, with visibility about 1½ miles and the temperature −2°C. The pilot was off station but agreed to board if we went inside the harbour. Halifax is an excellent natural harbour but, just as we approached the narrows and the point of no return, the pilot called on the VHF saying that the swell inside the harbour was too bad for him to board. The whole crew was disappointed as they had hoped that by hurrying through Halifax we might spend Christmas in port at Savannah. There was no option but to turn round and cruise outside until the gale diminished. We were lucky and at 1500 the wind shifted to north so we contacted the pilot who said the harbour was fairly calm during northerly winds. We wasted no time and moved into the harbour. Several other ships' sailings were delayed as they were gale-bound and now they demanded the use of the tugs first. We finally came alongside our berth at Autoport at 1900. Autoport is the Royal Canadian Navy's former seaplane base, and as its name implies handles all Halifax's car imports. It is across the river from Halifax and a taxi to town costs £3.

Leitch Transport of Toronto wanted to get the ship out of Halifax as quickly as possible, but the Halifax longshoremen or dockers refused to work after 1630, and with the temperature at −20°C no one could blame them. We spent the day around the shipping malls sampling the coffee, doughnuts and mince pie, which was made extremely sickly with the addition of bananas. At 1600 on 20th December we sailed from Halifax. The temperature was still −20°C but once clear of Nova Scotia it rose rapidly and reached 10°C. From Halifax we had the benefit of the Labrador Current which gave us a push along of nearly half a knot.

Along the American coast the navigational aids are poor. Unlike the Canadian coast, there is no Decca coverage. In fact, the whole coastline from Maine to Florida is as flat as a pancake, and indistinguishable by radar until 10 miles off. In the late afternoon gloom Nantucket light vessel was difficult to identify because, as we found, the relief vessel was on station and her radio signal was so weak as to be almost non-existent.

The way to Baltimore is through the Delaware River, which is also the way to Philadelphia. Fifty-four miles up the river the ship turns to port and goes for 23 miles through the Chesapeake Delaware Canal. In severe winters the canal is closed with ice and when this happens the way to Baltimore is through the entrance to Chesapeake Bay, 120 miles south of the Delaware. The canal was built in 1939 to make a short cut between Philadelphia and Baltimore. Then it was for single-ship traffic but in 1966 the canal was widened to 250 feet allowing ships going in the opposite direction to pass. Halfway along the canal the Delaware pilot is relieved by the Chesapeake Bay pilot and from the end of the canal to Baltimore is 40 miles.

One hour before arriving at the Delaware pilot a steering-motor solenoid burnt out. This meant that the ship could not steer so she was anchored until the fault was found and rectified. We could not afford to risk navigating the canal with imperfect steering. Five gangs of longshoremen were ordered for starting work at 1900 and we knew that we would be two hours late arriving. If the Volkswagens were not completely discharged by the evening of 23rd December the longshoremen had not the least intention of working Christmas Eve or Christmas Day, and two days of idleness would amount to a great many dollars in the ship's running costs.

A new bridge was being built across the Patapsco River at Baltimore and only one ship was allowed to pass at a time.

American Lancer, a United States Lines container ship, received priority so we waited. I remember having to take evasive action off Rotterdam in December 1968 because *American Lancer* charged at right angles on our port side, apparently unaware of the International Collision Rules. However, despite our setbacks work started at 2100 and my wife and I went ashore for her first American meal and a bottle of Californian wine.

We sailed from Baltimore at 1700 on 23rd December confident of spending Christmas Day alongside in Savannah. It is 155 miles down Chesapeake Bay to the sea, and the busiest man aboard was the cook preparing for Christmas. Savannah the crew regard as their home-from-home port and some have steady girl friends there.

At 0200 on Christmas morning a fuel pipe fractured so we had to stop for two hours to repair it. However, the pilots still boarded at 0800 and we steamed past Fort Pulaski at the mouth of the Savannah River. After seeing the port officials, agent, ship-chandler, repairman and trying unsuccessfully to telephone home, it was time for lunch. On Christmas Day the company permits a generous allowance to the crew — there was a free barrel of lager, with sherry, spirits, red and white wine and liqueurs. Dinner was a full-scale banquet with soups, prawn cocktail, smoked ham, fish, minute steak, turkey, ham, Christmas pudding, fruit salad, icecream, mincepies and Christmas cake, and some people managed a double portion of Christmas pudding. After lunch the cook and stewards have the rest of the day off, but first they leave a cold buffet out for those who may be hungry later on. The wives on board wore long dresses for the occasion and that night were kept busy dancing with the crew.

On Boxing Day the repairman, Nick the Greek, took a party of us out to lunch, choosing the Steak and Ale, which specialised in a salad bar. Afterwards we were invited to a party and then out to dinner.

Arctic Troll loaded liner board in Savannah — huge rolls of paper each weighing about 3 tons. At noon on 30th December we sailed for St John, New Brunswick. Although bound north, we were too far inshore to receive any help from the Gulf Stream until nearing Cape Hatteras. On New Year's Eve the sun shone brightly, picking out the deep blue of the Gulf Stream, and we could see distinctly where the Stream turned right and headed off towards Europe. This is a unique phenomenon and as the green cold water from the north is entered the sea's temperature drops 10° within minutes.

Hogmanay is as important to our Scots crew as Christmas and once more the company is extremely generous, donating another free barrel of lager and bottles of spirits. However, I welcomed the New Year in on the bridge as we ran into heavy rain. British law and the International Collision Rules insist that in such conditions we slow down and blow the whistle as in the days before radar. On New Year's night we passed Nantucket and sailed through a Russian fishing fleet of about 50 ships. On Friday afternoon, we arrived at St John. It was snowing and freezing. St John is a successful winter port when the river St Lawrence is closed. The 25-foot range of tide ensures that the port never freezes and one mile off-shore is a single point mooring for supertankers. The famous Reversing Falls proved to be disappointing. Nothing happened and the scenery was marred by a paper factory. Paper factories are the greatest of society's pollutants. The residue from the tree trunks is piped into the rivers and the fumes from the glue and sulphuric acid are allowed into the atmosphere. When downwind of them their smell is thoroughly obnoxious.

We sailed at 1700 on Monday, 5th January, with 14,000 tons of paper products. Normally, the final port is Stephenville on Newfoundland's west coast, but the paper mill was on strike so it was back to Dagenham. It was cold, still −20°C, and the temperature did not rise above freezing until we were 500 miles away from the Nova Scotia coast. Two hundred miles further on we passed over the spot where the *Titanic* sank after colliding with an iceberg on 12th April, 1912, with the loss of 1,513 lives.

Every time *Arctic Troll* puts to sea she participates in the Automated Mutual-Assistance Vessel Rescue System or AMVER. It is a system devised by the United States Coast Guard as a service to shipping. No charge is levied and ships of all nationalities are invited to participate. Approximately 1,100 ships are at sea in the North and South Atlantic at any one time. They report their position, course, speed and details of equipment aboard. For instance, if a doctor is aboard this important fact is reported to AMVER where all information is gathered and computerised. If any ship is in distress or needs medical assistance the AMVER plot shows instantly which ship is in the best position to render help. AMVER operates from Governor's Island New York harbour and the Coast Guard encourage seafarers to visit them.

The voyage across the Atlantic was unbelievably good, with no gales. The Decca navigator makes a landfall easy and we passed Bishop's Rock at 1800 on 12th January. Hundreds of ships have foundered near here, including in 1707, Admiral Sir Cloudesley Shovell's five-ship fleet homeward bound from Lisbon.

We berthed at Dagenham's riverside jetty at 2300 on 13th January to a reception of wives, children and girl friends.

Sea-wife
Sheila Seymour

Sitting under the hair-dryer in winter reading the society magazines one can usually find an article on cruising. Suggestions for one's new wardrobe will be made and advice given on tipping. The Canaries, Piraeus, Cyprus and Curaçao will be given a passing mention, and etiquette will be spelt out for those fortunate enough to sit at the captain's table. The ultimate in cruising is available, it will appear, to anyone with something in excess of £3,000 to spare. The accompanying advertisements will exhort one to seize this stupendous once-in-a-lifetime opportunity, even if it means sharing a cabin with three strangers.

So why not marry a captain and share his double bed as well as sit at his table? Those of us who have had the good sense to marry seafarers in the Merchant Navy can sail the seven seas at any time — and sail them on a shoestring. One of the things that is missing, however, is that glossy booklet provided to cruise passengers which gives a wealth of information on life at sea.

My sailing experience so far has been limited to three voyages aboard a 20,000-ton white-oil tanker, an elderly member of the tanker species, and so no doubt I still have much to learn. Moreover, my husband's company does not carry working wives, so the problems I have experienced may not be everybody's.

In spite of the Canaries, Piraeus, Cyprus and Curaçao — all of which have come my way — time can hang heavily on the sea-wife's hands and her greatest enemy is boredom. Inevitably, she will spend several hours alone each day while her husband is on watch. It is grand when there are several wives on board but usually there are only two or three and, unless their husbands are on identical watches, they may not see very much of one another. The shy wife who is unable to occupy herself easily will have problems and will soon return home.

Before my first voyage I met the wife of one of my husband's former shipmates. Since I knit, she told me to take plenty of wool. This was good advice since wool does not weigh much, and I have now extended knitting to dressmaking — four dresses this trip, including a long one. The luggage allowance does not permit of many books, but of course there is the Seafarers' Library on board. However, I strongly recommend a personal atlas, for one's geography improves by leaps and bounds at sea. A book on sea-birds is worth while, and I have found my French and Italian dictionaries invaluable in port.

The bar is open before lunch and in the evenings, and in the evenings too there are films or television cassettes. Darts, cribbage and liar dice are played, and there is sometimes a party or sing-song. There is no particular problem at these times. The sea-wife's problems arise during the morning and afternoon after she has cleaned her cabin and done her washing. It is a marvellous opportunity to learn, of course, and the College of the Sea will provide books and tuition as well as kits of different kinds. A wife on our last ship achieved a long-standing ambition by teaching herself to crochet. It is necessary for a wife to be able to achieve something during a voyage and to have a goal to aim at. Otherwise one can begin to feel like a parasite. It is good for one's morale to be able to make something useful and worth while.

On the night before the ship reaches port most bachelors and those married men whose wives are at home absent themselves from the bar to write letters. The sea-wife's husband is delighted to be relieved of this chore but the wife may take a different view of correspondence. Those who have never been to sea may not realise the importance to those of us at sea of receiving a regular flow of mail. Even in Europe the receipt of post can be spasmodic. Last month, after three whole weeks without mail, a delivery was made in Bremen — such an avalanche that it seemed like Christmas again.

I enjoy writing letters and take pleasure in corresponding with a Swedish friend and in writing to the children and staff of a Halifax secondary school, a link created by Ship Adoption. Ship Adoption is always looking for volunteers at sea who are willing to be matched with schools, for there are not enough ships to go round. In our company's fleet magazine I had read that several wives had joined the scheme. I write regularly to the school, sending postcards, maps and stamps, as I know that this material is displayed by the staff and, on a world map, the pupils trace our voyage, finding out about the countries we visit. A shipyard worker in Greece swapped stamps with us and thus we acquired a collection of more than 120 modern Greek stamps for the school. During my husband's leave we visit the school, showing our slides and being entertained. At Christmas we were delighted to attend the carol service, and my husband's employers now pay postage on the letters we send, which is an added incentive not to miss the post!

In port the sea-wife is indeed fortunate for she is not restricted by watchkeeping. Refineries, of course, are frequently sited in remote places and it is not always possible to get ashore, but during this trip our vessel spent three months in drydock at Skaramanga in Greece, not far from Athens. On our wedding anniversary my husband and I visited the Acropolis at dusk — a truly superb spectacle — and then ate a delicious meal in the Plaka. Our previous anniversary was celebrated by eating a French meal in Montreal.

White-oilers are frequently in port. On my first voyage the ship berthed at 54 ports in the following countries: the Canaries, UK, Eire, Sweden, Holland, Denmark, Portugal, Tunisia, Italy, Cyprus, the Lebanon (during the Yom Kippur war), France, Germany, Belgium and Norway — all in the five months and one week we were on board. My husband's employers now pay two air fares per year for wives, but these fares and the victualling allowance of £2.50 per week are set against the husband's income tax. By our reckoning if I were to stay at home in full-time employment we would be slightly better off financially than we are now but the separation would not be worth it. Many shipping companies now allow officers to take their children to sea as well as their wives.

At the risk of sounding like a TV commercial, I do urge all newly married wives to accompany their husbands to sea. One broadens one's horizons and at the same time appreciates one's own country more. Most seafarers put up with our presence very well and we are useful sometimes — 'Please can you put a new zip in my trousers?' 'Can you cut my hair?' or 'What else can I say to my girl friend in this letter?' Learning about life on the ocean wave is fun. There is always time for a joke — if the evening's spaghetti western is pathetic, the audience provide the humour, and any display of bare female flesh on celluloid is greeted by mating calls from frustrated matelots. Nor do you have to be a good sailor to go to sea — some of us are still sick in a slight swell and ready to die when it is rough for a few days, but life is sweeter than ever afterwards.

Having adapted to the life at sea so well, I now have another problem. How am I going to settle down ashore again to bring up those children we plan to have?

Down Tanker Alley
Ron Hawkins

Having rounded the Quoins we are in the Arabian Gulf and steaming well and truly down 'Tanker Alley'. The air is hot and bone-dry, just as if someone had opened an oven door. It dries the skin so quickly that you do not realise how much you are sweating. But fold your arms and protect a patch from the wind and it becomes wet and sticky with perspiration. It is weather to give you a tremendous thirst — and requiring regular large doses of salt tablets.

If any reader has never heard of the Quoins, they are familiar enough landmarks to tanker seamen. Looking astern one sees three bare and rocky islands, two of them wedge-shaped — hence Quoins. They sit there in three sizes, right in the middle of the Straits of Hormuz: Great Quoin Island, Little Quoin Island and Gap Island. On the most up-to-date Admiralty charts they are given their correct local names: As Salamah, Didimar and Fanaku. But I have yet to hear anyone say, 'We'll pass As Salamah in the morning.' It is always 'When do we get to the Quoins?'

Why Tanker Alley? Well, look at the ships coming towards us. They follow each other in a regular procession; by the time one is abeam the next is looming out of the heat haze ahead. And nearly every one of them is a tanker outward bound from the Gulf and deeply laden with crude oil. There is a tanker passing the Quoins every few minutes of the day and night.

A tanker differs from a cargo ship in that the decks are clear without any big hatches or masses of cargo gear. Most of these ships, however, are even more distinctive. As soon as a faint shadow emerges from the haze one notices its vast beam. Above that the accommodation towers like a block of high-rise flats. And, as they stretch out on either side, the bridge wings look indeed like wings, the wings of some huge bird hovering over the ship.

There was a time when a ship carried an air of individuality with her. A silhouette on the horizon was enough to indicate whether she was British or 'Scouwegian', just as once every great bridge was built differently, each one proclaiming the personality of its builder. Now one new suspension bridge looks much like the previous one, and so it is with these tankers. They all look much the same, whether British, Japanese, Liberian, Norwegian, or any other flag. If anyone has not guessed it, I am writing about VLCCs — Very Large Crude Carriers. Just as the design of great bridges has been reduced to the most efficient formula, so these ships have been built to do one particular job with the maximum efficiency. It is not surprising that they should all look very much the same and, like *Texaco Great Britain*, they will all eventually pass the Quoins because their job is to carry Middle East crude oil on long hauls around the world.

It is only since the 1950s that there has been any large-scale export of crude oil from the Middle East. My own career at sea has spanned the development of this trade. In 1951 my first ship, a tanker of 16,000 tons deadweight, was one of the biggest in the Company's fleet. Within a couple of years they had monsters twice that size and we were suitably impressed by the tales of those select few who had sailed on them.

But wonders soon become commonplace. Within a few more years the size of tankers had doubled again. It was the era of the super-tanker. By the end of the 1950s we were nonchalantly operating ships of 60,000 tons and giants of 100,000 tons were under construction.

Nor was that the end. The world's appetite for oil required ever more satisfying. With scarcely a pause for breath the shipyards started turning out tankers which had doubled in size yet again. These really were giants — of 200,000 tons and upwards, a completely new breed of ship. Even as an experienced seaman I must admit some feeling of awe when first I stepped on board one. I needed binoculars to recognise who was standing on the forecastle head.

The publicists must have been at a loss in coining a phrase to describe them. Having used up the word 'super' for ships a quarter of their size, what was left? Stupendous? Tremendous? 'Tremendous Tanker' has a certain ring to it. But this golden opportunity was missed and the unimaginative, if true, 'Very Large' was settled upon. Not 'Very Large Tanker', mark you, for these ships were crude carriers. Thus 'Very Large Crude Carriers', inevitably shortened to VLCC.

Size brought with it a considerable bonus. The operating costs of larger ships do not increase in the same proportion as their capacity. Therefore they are able to carry each ton of oil more cheaply. And at 200,000 tons deadweight, it becomes possible to carry oil round the Cape of Good Hope more cheaply than through the Suez Canal in smaller ships.

All this explains why *Texaco Great Britain* is inward bound to Ras Tanura to load a cargo of Saudi Arabian crude oil for discharge in Europe. Our full cargo is about 1,800,000 barrels or 63,000,000 gallons. I calculate that that much petrol would last the average car something like 190,000 years, or perhaps it would be more sensible to suggest that that much petrol would keep 190,000 average cars running for a year. But not all of our cargo of crude oil becomes petrol. The greater proportion of it will leave the refinery as heavier fuel oils.

About a week ago we received our orders from the owners by radio. The message read something like this: VOYAGE 3 LOAD RASTANURA SEGREGATED 350,000 BARRELS ARAB HEAVY BALANCE ARAB LIGHT DISCHARGE EUROPOORT STOP BUNKER RASTANURA SUFFICIENT REACH EUROPOORT PLUS RESERVE.

That is a straightforward enough cargo even though the message may seem a little obscure. We are instructed to load two different types of crude oil. Each oil field produces different oil, each with its special qualities, and a refinery will need to balance its intake of each kind with the products the market demands at the time. Three kinds of crude can be loaded at Ras Tanura, but our instructions are to load two. We will have to carry a quantity of heavier crude in separate tanks — a small quantity by comparison with the total cargo, no more than two tanks.

The barrel is a measure of volume. It can be said that our tanks hold so many barrels of oil when full to a certain level, but one cannot just say to the Mate, 'Fill her up'. Like all liquids, oil expands and contracts as its temperature varies, so a cargo loaded at 120°F will occupy a smaller volume when it cools to 80°F. As if by some magic we now have fewer barrels in the tanks than when the oil was loaded. Obviously, there has to be some standard measurement if our instructions are to make any sense and the barrels referred to in our orders are always nett barrels — that is, the volume occupied by the oil at 60°F.

There is another and more important reason why we cannot just pour oil into the tanks until they are full to the top. Oil has weight as well as volume and it is this weight that brings the ship down to her marks. She can only carry so many tons before sinking gracefully beneath the waves. The Mate would feel rather foolish if he filled the tanks with so many nett barrels that he found the water lapping round his feet on deck. It is not as easy as driving a car into a filling station and saying, 'Fill her up'.

Before loading can be carried out careful calculations in terms of both barrels and tons have to be made.

As everyone knows, to say that a ship is 'down to her marks' means that she is loaded to the draught permitted by the Plimsoll Mark on her side. There are, indeed, a number of Plimsoll lines at different levels to indicate how deeply we can load in summer, winter or tropical conditions. And on the chartroom bulkhead there is a chart of the world showing the areas and seasons where each line applies. When loaded to the appropriate load line the ship is considered to have enough buoyancy to meet the expected weather conditions.

We have, therefore, to calculate how many tons will load the ship down to the governing load line. It is not just a matter of seeing that she is down to the appropriate Plimsoll mark for the loading port. If there are winter conditions anywhere along our route we must be sure that the ship is not overloaded as she enters that zone. It often happens that the amount of cargo loaded at Ras Tanura depends on the ship's arrival off the Spanish coast at her winter marks a month later.

The tonnage that will take her down to her marks is known as the deadweight, and having calculated the deadweight we are well on the way to deciding just how much cargo is required. A further stage is necessary because the deadweight includes the various supplies the ship must carry round with her. The bunkers that we need to reach Europoort safely come to about 7,000 tons. Then there are stores, lub-oil and fresh water, all of which account for at least another 600 tons. After making deductions for these we arrive at the cargo figure.

At last I can order the required quantity in tons or barrels. The same cable will include any requests I have for the attention of the agent. At the end of the voyage they will not be many, perhaps just a few fresh stores, though at this time of the year they are expensive and in short supply. Temperatures of 110°F in the shade are not ideal for growing salads and vegetables. Many people on board will think that the most important thing is to ensure an exchange of films and TV tapes.

Meanwhile the Mate's calculations are far from finished. Some of the most important of them have yet to be made and for these we look to electronic aids or, in most modern ships, to a full computer. Even at this stage it would be foolhardy just to load the necessary amount of cargo into the tanks indiscriminately. Unless it is evenly distributed dangerous stresses might occur in the ship's structure. The two stresses we are most concerned about are caused by bending moments and shear forces.

If too much weight is concentrated at the ends of the ship they will try to sink lower in the water while the more buoyant midships section will tend to float higher. Similarly if the greater part of the weight is concentrated amidships it is that part of the ship which will tend to sink lower in the water. These are known as hogging and sagging stresses. They really do bend the ship, though within limits there is no need to be concerned because the designer expects it to happen and all ships are constructed so as to allow some flexibility. It is quite usual to find that we have sagged up to six inches on completion of loading. And when the ship is working in a seaway you can stand and watch the expansion joints on the deck pipelines moving that much.

The shear stresses occur much more locally. If adjacent tanks contain vastly different amounts of cargo there will be a similar difference in their buoyancy: the heavier will try to sink much lower in the water. There will consequently be a force trying to crack the ship in two at the bulkhead between them.

Somehow the cargo has to be arranged in the tanks so that these stresses remain within safe limits throughout the voyage. The situation changes on passage because bunkers are burnt and cargo and bunkers have to be transferred to maintain a good trim. The heavy crude parcel has had to be segregated in separate tanks. Often we have to discharge at two ports, and sometimes we load at two different ports with even more segregated grades. No wonder the Mate needs rather more than just paper and pencil when he makes his calculations.

Ras Tanura might be described as the world's biggest filling-station. 'Ras' is Arabic for headland, but it is difficult to distinguish this low sandy spit of land. The shoreline is cluttered with oil tanks, gas spheres, and ships at loading jetties. It is a science fiction landscape of weaving pipes and the weird columns of 'Cat Crackers'. There are flares of burning gases flying like banners, and great clouds of black smoke climb lazily from the chimneys to spread out like an umbrella above it all.

It is hot outside. Even in the air-conditioned wheelhouse you can feel the heat being reflected from the burnished surface of the sea. Walk outside and it hits you with almost physical force. And there is not much relief to be gained from a dip in the swimming-pool. With the sea temperature over 90°F, it is rather like bathing in pea-soup.

The berths for the VLCCs are on the Sea Island. This is a long jetty with four berths on either side and it is situated in deep water nearly three miles offshore. So there is no chance of any shore leave. Not that there are many moans about that. Everyone's greatest wish is for a fast load and a quick turn round.

Little time is wasted. Within an hour of our lines going ashore the cargo hoses are connected and loading begins. But for the first few hours there is little sign of the ship sinking deeper in the water for, although some tanks are being filled, the ballast is being pumped out of others just as quickly. In the main the cargo operations are directed from a central control-room. Most of the valves and pumps can be remotely operated from here and dials display the level of oil in each tank.

However, loading the ship is not just a matter of sitting in air-conditioned comfort while the oil flows through the pipelines and into the tanks. The mate on watch has plenty of jobs to attend to on deck. Safety and pollution checks must be made, moorings and gangway attended to, gas vents adjusted, and the valves and gauges themselves often have to be checked visually. During the course of a six-hour cargo watch the duty mate must cover a considerable distance, for it is a good three-minute walk, for instance, to the forecastle-head. This problem was not overlooked when VLCCs were a novelty. It was decided that bicycles would be necessary to cover the distance. Unfortunately, seamen proved prone to cycle accidents. Several broken limbs later, they now make their rounds on foot.

The mood on board changes once loading is completed. The day after leaving Ras Tanura we pass the Quoins again. This time we are in the procession of loaded tankers and we can sympathise with those just beginning to feel the blast-furnace heat of the Gulf. The next day Ras-al-Hadd is abeam and the weather cools down with a rush. We head out into the Arabian Sea and the south-west monsoon. It is invigorating to lean over the bridge wing and feel the first puff of cool breeze on your face. For the next month the ship settles into the steady routine of watch-keeping and maintenance.

From Ras Tanura to Europoort is 11,550 miles. It involves following a course which sweeps in great arcs right round the continent of Africa. During the voyage we will experience as many seasons as the weeks it will take. From the humid winds of the monsoon, through the winter gales of the Cape, on to the mild spring of the South Atlantic and the brief journey through the tropics, to the summer of the North Atlantic. There is no lack of variety in our weather.

Although the distance between the two ports is calculated accurately in miles, not many people on board talk of it in that way. Mileage is of most interest to the Chief Engineer when calculating the amount of bunkers required, and to the Second Mate for estimating our time of arrival or ETA. It is this ETA that interests most people. For the seaman distance usually becomes time. When a new set of orders is received he does not think, 'That's another 11,000 miles to steam,' but 'That will take us thirty-four days.' And as the voyage progresses nobody asks,

'How much further to go?' but 'When are we due?' It is logical because 11,000 miles will seem a lot further to a seaman sailing on a 12-knot ship than it will to one sailing on a 15-knot ship.

After the first of the monsoon the breeze soon freshens, with a good chance of a gale. Between the beginning of June and the end of August these conditions can be guaranteed. Over much of the world the weather is not so variable and unpredictable as it is in England. Most of the weather in England is dictated by the uncertain habits of the Atlantic depressions. But much of our steaming is through the great wind systems of the world that blow regularly year after year without fail. It was this that made many of the oceanic voyages by sailing ship possible. It also held back many voyages of discovery until the secrets were learned. Today it gives the modern seaman a chance to plan the shipboard maintenance. Even when we leave Ras Tanura the Mate knows that any scaling and painting on the main deck will have to wait for the fine weather of the Trades after Capetown.

Modern ships do not have to wait for a fair wind, but no more than the old explorers can their seamen afford to ignore the weather. You may think that a ship the size of a VLCC would be safe from any but the biggest seas, but this is far from the case. It is a matter of two obstinate giants meeting head on. Water is incompressible and will not give way. The very bulk of a VLCC gives it momentum that tends to drive the ship right through the seas instead of rising gracefully over them. For our own good we must give way a little. As the wind freshens I am alert to how the ship moves in the seaway and quick to ease the engines as soon as we start hitting the seas.

These are largely days of routine for our job has been reduced to its simplest aspect. We need only to ensure that our 250,000 tons of crude oil are transported safely and efficiently. Each little mark on the chart records our orderly progress — from noon to evening star sights, to morning star sights, and on to the next noon. A brief stop off Capetown is the only break we can look forward to. Here the ship will rendezvous with a launch to pick up mail, change our films and TV tapes, and take on fresh provisions. The order of priority should be noted. We gulp down the much-needed draught of tonic, and are off again along the well-worn courses of the second part of the passage.

Of course it is not really quite as simple as that; nor as tedious; often it is not quite so routine. Our cargo must be transported safely and we cannot just sit around and expect this to happen. The work of the regular watchkeepers is most closely concerned with it on this passage. Every hour of the day they will be making a decision or taking some precaution, either in navigating the vessel or operating the machinery, to ensure a safe passage. But beyond this immediate responsibility, to have it done efficiently requires a considerable amount of work. Without regular maintenance machinery and equipment will not work when it is required, and even the ship's structure will deteriorate unless it is properly looked after. Ships are not just painted to make them look beautiful. Rust is a sign that the steel beneath it is being eaten away and weakened. Operating a modern ship, and getting her from one port to another, is a complex business requiring careful planning and cooperation both on board and ashore.

Eventually, about a month after leaving Ras Tanura, we approach Ushant and the English Channel. Not so long ago it was about here that seamen would go down with that highly infectious disease known as 'The Channels'. The symptoms are a lighthearted and devil-may-care attitude to life. The sufferer becomes somewhat restless, dividing his time between trying to cram twice as much into a suitcase as it was designed to hold and racing round the ship trying to find a railway timetable. Because we do not nowadays go on leave together, and may fly home from anywhere, there has been a marked decline in the incidence of this disease in recent years and it is not nearly as contagious as formerly.

If you are serving on a VLCC the approach to Ushant is likely to herald the beginning of the busiest part of the whole voyage, with never a thought of going home. As master, it certainly means that my responsibilities become real and tangible. There are bound to be long and arduous hours on the bridge even in the best of weather. To the holiday-maker walking along the Leas at Folkestone the Dover Straits may seem a large expanse of water — 24 miles or so may seem quite wide enough even for a ship of this size. But the sandbanks are invisible to the holiday-maker and it is our draught of 65 feet that is crucial. Below the waterline we extend as far as a seven-storey building is high. The navigation is onerous but not particularly difficult because a considerable array of aids is provided. Buoys, lightvessels, coastal landmarks and lighthouses, radio and radar beacons, the Decca navigation system, and our own radar can all be used to fix the vessel's position. And it is necessary to know our exact position at any instant since, although I have the advantage of having them marked on the chart, those sandbanks are just as invisible to me as they are to the holiday-maker.

The other great problem is the traffic. Something like 700 ships a day pass Dover. The situation has been simplified in recent years by the introduction of a Traffic Separation Scheme, which means that the ships are separated into lanes on either side of the Channel as if they were using a dual carriageway road. At least, that is the theory, but as yet there are no proper traffic policemen, so there is always somebody who insists on proving his independence and cannot do it without annoying — or endangering — other people. Imagine the results if a driver tried to take his car down the wrong lane of the M1! Such ships are labelled rogues by the coastguard; we sometimes have less proper names for them on the bridge.

With the fixing of the ship's position, avoiding other ships, and cursing some little coaster weaving an erratic course through the route reserved for deep-draughted vessels, both I and the officer of the watch are kept fully occupied. Should the weather close in all this requires even more care and vigilance. In addition a continuous radar watch must be kept and the echoes of other ships plotted to discover what they are doing and how much of a threat they are to our safety. There can easily be more than 50 ships on the screen within a 12-mile range, so alertness and experience must be combined to ensure that any ship likely to pass dangerously close is not missed at an early stage. This is an area of modern ship operation where electronics and computers have a big contribution to make to safety.

Europoort exists: it is not just a name dreamed up for our destination. It is the modern extension of the old Dutch port of Rotterdam, and in this case 'extension' is literally true. Having already made a good part of their country for themselves, the Dutch are still pushing it further and further out into the North Sea. Europoort is built on a vast area of reclaimed land at the mouth of the river Maas. Nor is that the limit of Dutch industry: beyond that again they have dredged a channel — the Eurochannel, of course — forty miles out to sea in order to get the big tankers into their port.

As befits our size, we have preferential treatment. While lesser ships have to mill about the pilot boat, jostling for a turn to ship a pilot, our pilot arrives in the middle of the North Sea and by helicopter. Nor should it prove a surprise to learn that we need two pilots. One is sufficient to pilot the ship but his partner is fully occupied with communications. Perhaps it will seem just as inevitable when I reveal that they are both of a size proportionate to the ship, though that is coincidental. All Dutch pilots seem to be big men, with correspondingly large appetites. On a bridge the size of ours they appear in proportion; cooped up in the wheelhouse of a coaster they must be more uncomfortable.

As we approach the busy river entrance our progress becomes positively regal. We glide serenely along while ahead of us scurries a patrol boat, shooing away any smaller vessels that might stray in our path. The flashing blue light at its masthead gives it an air of importance. Finally we gather a whole retinue of tugs around us to heave and fuss and eventually to ease us alongside the berth.

Time to relax after all that, you may think. To relax! There is scarcely time to catch your breath. As soon as the gangway is down people pour on board. The ship is suddenly crowded with strangers and I must start dealing with the business for this port. Customs and immigration officials are asking for crew lists, declaration forms and store-lists. The port health authority needs the ship's de-rat certificate and the crew vaccination books. The agent requires more crew lists and lots of other information. I have to arrange for crew members to visit the doctor and the dentist and — most important once more — I must not forget to arrange for an exchange of films and TV tapes. The cargo consignees are somewhere in the crowd asking for the bills of lading and the notice of readiness. And now the agent wants the ship's register, safety equipment, safety radio and SAFCON certificates in order to obtain clearance outwards. We have not even started discharging the cargo yet.

The first hectic rush of activity subsides. The officials pack up their papers and go. At last I have time to read my mail from home, and then I intend to catch up on my sleep. If anyone expects to hear lurid tales of Jack rushing ashore to hit the night spots after months at sea he is going to be disappointed.

Meanwhile, there is still plenty happening. The most important operation, of course, is to discharge our precious cargo of crude oil. It is almost, but not quite, the reverse procedure to loading the ship, the 'not quite' part being that it will be pumped ashore using the ship's own pumps. To do it within a reasonable time is no small undertaking. There are four pumps which together are capable of pumping the oil ashore at more than 10,000 tons an hour. To drive them at that speed needs a lot of power — almost as much horsepower as driving the ship through the water at full speed. Our boilers have no more rest than the crew in port; they have to steam just as hard as at sea.

Before our arrival the mate will have planned the discharge with as much care as he did the loading. He has to find a solution to a similar equation: each grade needs to be discharged separately so as to avoid any dangerous shear and bending stresses and so as to keep the vessel trimmed well by the stern to assist in draining the tanks. Then, at some stage, water ballast must be loaded into those tanks from which oil has already been discharged.

Finally, but by no means least, the ship must be provisioned and stored for the next voyage. We cannot rely on the chief steward nipping round to the supermarket just before we sail. He has to shop for 56 people, and it is his only chance to stock up for, perhaps, three months. Our stores department in London supply the experience: they will have arranged the storing long before we arrived, and most likely the stores themselves will have been sent across the Channel in containers to avoid higher continental prices. There is not only our food to be taken on board. Spare parts, tools, paints, ropes and ship chandlery are all required as well if we are to carry the next cargo safely and efficiently.

Now we have to start steaming all those 11,550 miles back to Ras Tanura, only now no more than a third of our tanks are filled — with water ballast — and our draught is only half of what it was when loaded. This is always the busiest half of the voyage as we prepare for the next cargo. And somewhere between Europoort and Ras Tanura we will have to perform a conjuring trick. At the moment we have dirty ballast water on board that has been loaded straight into tanks that still had the residue of the cargo in them. But when we arrive at Ras Tanura pure, clean water will be pumped over the side with no fear of pollution. Just as important, not one drop of oil will have been pumped into the sea in between times.

It is not really a difficult trick when you can see behind the scenes. Success depends on two simple facts: that oil and water do not mix easily and will soon separate, oil being the lighter floats on top of the water. If they did not dislike each other quite as much as they do or if oil were heavier than water then the trick would not work. As it is, tankers can safely use the load-on top procedure to clean their tanks and avoid pollution.

As a first step at least enough tanks must be cleaned to take the clean ballast water. They are washed very easily and thoroughly with high-pressure water jets from machines permanently fixed inside the tanks themselves.

This is the point at which to mention one of the most important procedures in operating VLCCs — the control of the atmosphere inside the tanks. In 1969 there were three explosions in VLCCs, all within a few weeks and all during the time they were washing tanks. The oil industry then launched a massive research programme to discover the cause. The conclusion was that static electricity must be in some way to blame. But on board the ships it is not easy to apply this knowledge, for the very act of washing tanks builds up very high charges of static. If that could not be prevented, the only other solution was to ensure that it could not cause an explosion. At first that may seem even more difficult but an easy means of doing it had been going to waste up the funnel ever since there had been tankers. Fire — and an explosion is no more than a violent fire — must have oxygen to live. The funnel gases do not contain oxygen, for it has been burnt already to provide the fires in the boilers. All that remains is to blow 'inert' gas into the tanks to replace the normal air in them. After that, no matter what petroleum vapours are given off by the oil and no matter how much the static flashes around like a vivid lightning display, there cannot be an explosion. Throughout the voyage, therefore, we follow procedures to ensure that the atmosphere in the tanks does not contain oxygen — it is inert.

Having eliminated the danger of explosion, there is another problem that must be solved. As the tanks are being washed the dirty water that accumulates must be pumped out of them. The problem is where to put it, for we cannot pump it over the side and cause pollution. It is easy enough though to put it in another tank. These are the slop tanks and the dirty water can be left safely in them for a while until the oil and water have worked out their differences. The oil always comes out on top. As the suction is at the bottom of the tank, we can carefully pump out the clean water, making sure the pump is stopped just before the layer of oil is reached.

A similar procedure can be used to deal with dirty ballast. By now the oil will have separated from that, so most can be pumped overboard. The final few feet are treated in the same way as the wash water — stripped back into the slop tanks to allow further separation.

Notice that we have not lost any oil; it has only been moved from the ballast tanks to the slop tanks. On a normal voyage we will probably find that more than 500 tons has been handled in this way. It may be regarded as a symbolic tank of oil in this modern world. Not only does it represent that much less pollution in the sea but it is also a similar amount of energy conserved, for it will be mixed with the next cargo when we load it. Hence the description 'Load-on-top'.

To go back a little along our course line, when the tanks have been cleaned and blown out with fresh air it is time to enter them for inspection and to carry out any repairs that may be necessary.

It is quite a journey to the bottom of one centre, our biggest tank, but one well worth making. If a VLCC ever becomes a tourist attraction it will provide the high spot for most visits. To reach this high spot, however, you start with a long climb down — it seems an even longer climb up! There are just about 90 feet of open iron-rung ladders to negotiate, so it is best to concentrate on each rung as it comes and not to look down — or up. Once at the bottom you can stand and look round the vast structure. I think it is the best place in which to gain an impression of the vessel's size. The great deck area soon shrinks from familiarity, but the steel structure inside the tanks never loses its impact.

These tanks have been likened to cathedrals and that is how the sight always strikes me. In size alone it makes a respectable nave for any cathedral. And the resemblance is enhanced by the massive columns of the deep frames and the rays of sunlight slanting across the tank. You also gain a similar feeling of quiet and isolation from the outside world down there. You can stand still and hear little more than the gentle swish of the water passing the hull.

There is no opportunity to stand around for long. If all is in order it is time to climb back up to the bustle on deck and get the ballast change started. With all this activity the time tends to pass more quickly on the ballast passage than when we are loaded. The orders for the next voyage have been received and the ship's routine for the next couple of months has been fixed once more. The mate must start his calculations and I must send a message to Ras Tanura. It is not long before we see the familiar shapes of the Quoins ahead of us, only this time the heat that awaits us in the Gulf does not seem such a menace. In fact I think I feel a touch of the Channels coming on as I will definitely be going home from Ras Tanura; the cable arrived last night. Considering where we are, perhaps it is an attack of the Gulfs I am suffering from.

Please pass the salt tablets. Where did I leave my suitcases? Surely somebody must know the times of the flights to Heathrow!

All in the Day's Work
Edwin Gregson

At 2100 on 31st January 1979, in position 33° 39' North 46° 13' West, *Jamaica Producer* received from Greek Flag mv *Mitsos* a distress message that she had a hole in Number 3 Starboard (Wing Tank) and the pumps were not pumping out the water. The list was 10 degrees and she required tug assistance. *Jamaica Producer* set course to rendezvous with her on 1st February.

By 0531 both ships were steaming together at reduced speeds and at 0812 and 0943 contact was made with *Mitsos* who was awaiting instructions from Athens. The weather was gale force westerly winds with a rough sea and heavy swell. At 1039, *Mitsos* advised that they were abandoning ship. *Jamaica Producer* closed in towards *Mitsos* and lifeboats were cleared away, and pilot ladder and scrambling nets, boat rope and lifebuoys were prepared on the port side. Because of the heavy swell *Mitsos*, with a starboard list, intended to use only the starboard lifeboat and one liferaft but on releasing the raft the line parted and it drifted away upside down.

Between 1158 and 1250, when *Jamaica Producer* was abeam of *Mitsos*, three rocket lines were fired from *Mitsos*. The first one missed but the other two were received on board. The lines attached to them parted due to the long bight in the water between the ships and the heavy swell. At 1301, *Mitsos* launched her starboard lifeboat with some crew members on board, but to prevent damage to the boat in the heavy swell it was not possible to lie alongside and the boat lay just astern of *Mitsos* on a boat rope. This meant that the remainder of the crew had to jump into the water and swim to the lifeboat with a guide rope. During this operation, the sixteen-year-old messboy was carried away in the swell. A lookout was kept from *Jamaica Producer*, but he was not sighted.

At 1405, the lifeboat was let go from *Mitsos* and drifted clear. By then mv *Nordic Louisiana*, a tanker, had arrived on the scene and made an attempt to approach the lifeboat, but was unsuccessful. Mv *Cordillera Express*, a German container ship, also arrived to assist.

At 1450 *Jamaica Producer* resumed manoeuvring to approach the lifeboat and at 1500 a rocket was fired, but it missed the lifeboat. By 1542, the lifeboat was alongside on the port side. It was ranging heavily up and down the ship's side in the heavy swell. At 1545 the first survivor was aboard. All crew members of *Jamaica Producer* were standing by on deck to assist. The scrambling nets were found to be the most effective aid, and as the *Mitsos* crew grabbed hold of them, they were heaved up bodily and assisted onto the deck. There was one lady, the chief officer's wife/stewardess. Captain Dimitros was the last survivor of 26 to come on board.

Nordic Louisiana and *Cordillera Express* had formed up to carry out a pattern search for the missing mess boy and *Jamaica Producer* took her place. He was sighted at 1710, but when the vessel was turned round he was lost in the swell. He was sighted later, but lost sight of again. Knowing that he was still alive the other ships closed in and the search was continued after darkness. At 1823 lifebuoys with marker lights were dropped in the area. *Jamaica Producer* used her Aldis lamp and *Cordillera Express* her searchlight. A whistle was heard close to one of the marker lights and after further manoeuvring the boy was again sighted and brought alongside on the port side. He was hauled on board at 2025 and taken immediately to the hospital to be treated for shock by the stewardess. This was after 6 hours 41 minutes in the water.

The Greek Ministry of Marine enquired and were advised that the entire crew of 27 had been rescued. At the last daylight sighting of mv *Mitsos* she was listing heavily to starboard and on clearing the area, latitude 36° 04' North longitude 44° 21' West, there was no radar target showing. *Mitsos* had a cargo of scrap metal from Newark NJ to Salonika.

The Marine Society

The Marine Society is the world's oldest maritime charity. It was founded in 1756 by Jonas Hanway, with the active interest of Sir John Fielding, to encourage men to volunteer for service in the fleet at the outbreak of the Seven Years War. In 1786 it established a pattern of nautical education — the training ship — which lasted for more than 150 years. Since the Second World War it has led the way in establishing higher educational standards for the Merchant Navy officer, and, in its sponsorship of the Nautical Institute, has helped to inaugurate still higher professional standards. In 1976 The Marine Society amalgamated with the Seafarers Education Service and College of the Sea, which had itself absorbed the work of the British Ship Adoption Society in the previous year. On the closure of the Red Ensign Club (where Conrad stayed) the Society also took over the management of the London School of Nautical Cookery.

The London School of Nautical Cookery was the first school to train ships' cooks. Ship Adoption pioneered contacts between schools and seafarers, bringing home to those at school Britain's dependence upon the sea. The Seafarers Education Service — founded in 1919 by Albert Mansbridge — established the Merchant Navy's library service and, through its College of the Sea, provided seafarers with facilities for their general education. All these activities are carried on nowadays from the Society's London headquarters at 202 Lambeth Road in handsome premises which face Archbishop's Park.

In 1981 the Society successfully launched MAST (the Marine Adventure Sailing Trust), a £1,050,000 investment trust which aims to help the Training Ship *Foudroyant* and other sail training associations.

The modern Marine Society is concerned, as its founders were, with helping to provide Britain with fine seafarers. Today its activities impinge upon the seafarer's well-being from the time when his or her thoughts first turn to the sea to the time when he or she has resettled successfully on land, whether this resettlement comes in retirement or on returning ashore earlier in life. The Society has always enjoyed the reigning monarch's patronage, King George II subscribing £1,000 when the Society was first established.